MW00911641

THE WRITE BRIDGE
| MIND THE GAP |
A Biannual Literary Journal

Copyright © 2023 by Anamcara Press LLC
https://anamcara-press.com/the-write-bridge-zine/
Published biannually
Subscriptions: https://anamcara-press.com/subscribe-to-the-journal/
Cover and Book design by Maureen Carroll
Editors Maureen Carroll, Amber Fraley, Ronda Miller
Arial, Tomarik, Lato, Professor Minty
Printed in the United States of America.

Book description: 2023 Journal anthology

This periodical is devoted to literature in a broad sense, publishing short stories, poetry, plays, and essays, along with book reviews, biographical profiles of authors, interviews and occasional letters. The essays in this journal are works of creative nonfiction. The fiction in this journal are products of the author's imaginations or are used fictitiously and are not to be construed as real. Any resemblance to actual events, locales, organizations or persons, living or dead, is entirely coincidental.

Published by
ANAMCARA PRESS LLC
P.O. Box 442072, Lawrence, KS 66044
https://anamcara-press.com

Ordering Information: Quantity sales. Special discounts are available on quantity purchases for libraries, bookstores, and others. For details, contact the publisher at the address above.

CATALOGING DATA:
THE WRITE BRIDGE JOURNAL / Perilous & Playful / Issue 5: Summer 2023
[edited by] Maureen Carroll [and] Amber Fraley [and] Ronda Miller

ISBN-13: The Write Bridge Journal Summer 2023, 978-1-960462-20-6
ISSN: Pending
LCO010000 LITERARY COLLECTIONS / Essays
LCO020000 LITERARY COLLECTIONS / Interviews
HUM003000 HUMOR / Form / Essays
BIO026000 BIOGRAPHY & AUTOBIOGRAPHY / Personal Memoirs

"Lady,
We perform before Thee,
Walking a joyous discipline,
A thin thread of courage,
A slim high wire of dependence
Over abysses."

"Acrobat's Song" an excerpt from "Circus of the Sun" —Robert Lax

PREVIOUS ISSUES OF THE WRITE BRIDGE

THE WRITE BRIDGE | MIND THE GAP | FALL 2022
JOURNAL ISSUE #4
Theme: Fortitude and Pusillanimity

THE WRITE BRIDGE | MIND THE GAP | SPRING 2022
JOURNAL ISSUE #3
Theme: Heartbreak And Desire

THE WRITE BRIDGE | MIND THE GAP | FALL 2021
JOURNAL ISSUE #2
Theme: Isolation And Emergence

THE WRITE BRIDGE | MIND THE GAP | SPRING 2021
JOURNAL ISSUE #1
Authors explore the topic of inclusion, and offer up
some pandemic prose.

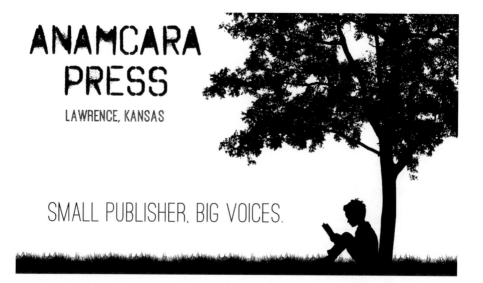

ANAMCARA
PRESS
LAWRENCE, KANSAS

SMALL PUBLISHER, BIG VOICES.

THE WRITE BRIDGE

| *MIND THE GAP* |

A Biannual Literary Journal

SELECT WORKS OF NON-FICTION, POETRY, FICTION & ART

ISSUE #5; SUMMER 2023

PERILOUS and PLAYFUL

Anamcara Press LLC | Lawrence, Kansas

Our mission is to spark wonder. *The Write Bridge* is published twice a year and features enthralling poetry, short fiction, and creative nonfiction.

WELCOME TO
THE WRITE BRIDGE JOURNAL

In each edition of *The Write Bridge* readers are encouraged to "mind the gap" as writers and artists with powerful voices explore topics that broaden our thinking.

In a 1936 Esquire article entitled "The Crack Up," author F. Scott Fitzgerald wrote:

> *"Before I go on with this short history, let me make a general observation—the test of a first-rate intelligence is the ability to hold two opposed ideas in the mind at the same time, and still retain the ability to function. One should, for example, be able to see that things are hopeless and yet be determined to make them otherwise. This philosophy fitted on to my early adult life, when I saw the improbable, the implausible, often the 'impossible,' come true."*

The Write Bridge pushes at the boundaries, presenting authors and readers with two concepts to explore, as in *Perilous* and *Playful*, the themes for *The Write Bridge* Journal Summer 2023 edition.

THE WRITE BRIDGE JOURNAL STAFF

Meet the team!

Anamcara Press LLC was founded by Maureen "Micki" Carroll in 2014 in celebration of art and community, and in support of authors and artists in their creative endeavors.

Carroll is a writer, educator, graphic designer, and all around cat herder. Her first book, *A Wyoming Cowboy in Hitler's Germany* combines war era correspondence and 70 year old photographs to depict an age of heroism and innocence. *The Tree Who Walked Through Time* was published in collaboration with 17 artists, including crop artist Stan Herd. She is also the author of the middle-grade series, Jo & the School's Out Squad. Carroll Co-Chairs Kansas Authors Club District #2.

Assistant Editor and Publicist, Amber Fraley is your typical Gen Xer suburban Kansas wife and mom of one who grew up a book nerd in a dysfunctional family and now writes about those experiences as hilarious therapy. She's the author of the humorous essay collection *From Kansas, Not Dorothy*, and the viral essay "Gen X Will Not Go Quietly," as well as numerous human interest articles. Amber loves Kansas with all her heart, is frequently awkward in public, and desperately wishes to see a tornado and live to tell the tale.

Art/Design Editor, Kathleen (Kat) Williams is a multi-disciplinary artisan and scholar. Mythologist, metalsmith, seamstress, and songstress, Kat loves all things creative. With ample degrees in Arts and Culture she brings a diversified aesthetic to the publications of Anamcara Press. When she's not writing new myths or hand-crafting adornments, she's singing songs and helping other writers with their websites. You can find more about her and her work at www.tb3f.com

Ronda Miller, Poetry Editor, is a Life Coach specializing in trauma. Miller teaches The Importance of Voice for Trauma Transformation in concert with The Johnson County Library, School of Trades and Department of Corrections. Her five books of poetry include: *Going Home: Poems from My Life*, *MoonStain*, *WaterSigns*, *Winds of Time* and *I Love the Child*. Miller was state President for Kansas Authors Club, 2018 – 2019, and currently sits on the Board of The Writers Place where she is committee chair (at risk teen poetry classes) for the yearly In Our Own Words anthology.

Alisha Ashley is a digital marketing strategist and campaign coordinator with fifteen years' experience in social justice and advocacy work. She writes short stories, poetry, and contemplative essays on politics, organizing for societal change, and trauma recovery. She holds a Bachelor's degree in Political Science from the University of Kansas and a Strategic Planning Certificate from UC Berkeley. She lives in Lenexa, KS with her husband Scott and their dog, Everett.

CONTRIBUTING VISUAL ARTISTS

 Jospeh Maino Joseph Maino is a freelance fine art, portrait and event photographer currently based in Reno, Nevada. He has made images for Kansas City.com and *The Independent magazine* and currently shoots for *The Fernley Reporter* newspaper. He displays his art at the Art Indeed Gallery and other venues around Reno. His work may be viewed at www.JosephMainoPhoto.com.

 Cathy Martin is a mixed-media artist who lives and works on ten acres of woodland and meadow in the rolling hills of beautiful NE Kansas. Surrounded by the rich color and tapestry of the Colorado mountains and Iowa farmlands in her youth, landscapes are her specialty, and Cathy enjoys adding various wildlife into many of her paintings.

 Ronda Miller, Poetry Editor, is a Life Coach specializing in trauma. Miller teaches The Importance of Voice for Trauma Transformation in concert with The Johnson County Library, School of Trades and Department of Corrections. Her five books of poetry include: *Going Home: Poems from My Life, Moon-Stain, WaterSigns, Winds of Time* and *I Love the Child.*

 Diana Dunkley Is a full-time artist working out of Studio 3D in Lawrence, KS USA for over 40 years. Diana received a B.F.A. from the University of Kansas with a double degree in Sculpture and Interior Design. Dunkley's work is shown nationally and internationally, including exhibitions in Ottawa, Canada and Sydney and Katoomba, Australia. Dunkley has also exhibited in multiple solo and group exhibitions and is in collections around the globe.

Barbara Waterman-Peters, (BFA, Washburn University, MFA, Kansas State University, Honorary Doctor of Fine Arts, Washburn University) taught at Washburn and Kansas State Universities as well as for Lassen Community College in California. She has received a Certificate of Recognition for Outstanding Achievement from the State of Kansas and the Monroe Award from the Washburn University Alumni Association. In 2011 she was awarded the ARTY for Distinguished Visual Artist from ARTS Connect in Topeka. Her work has been included in more than 300 solo, group and juried exhibits. She is represented by several galleries, Jones in Kansas City, SNW in Manhattan, and Beauchamp in Topeka. She owns STUDIO 831 in the North Topeka Arts & Entertainment District (NOTO).

Amanda McCollum, Overland Park, Kansas-based illustrator and graphic designer Amanda McCollum has been working in the arts since 2010. While working as a face painter, caricature artist, and letter brush artist at the Walt Disneyland Resort, she spent much of her time outside, observing the small (and occasionally large) wildlife that humans share space with. Amanda's work was most recently featured in the Litha group show at Gallery Athanor in Kansas City, MO. and in the Her Art/Their Art group show at Interurban Art House in Overland Park, KS. She grew up in the Chicagoland area, where she earned her Bachelor's Degree in graphic design.

Bobbie attended KU and stayed in Lawrence KS for 17 years creating, showing, and selling mixed media art, children book illustrations, drawings, and paintings. A member of art co-op groups Dot Dot Dot and Quintessential 5, Bobbie has had shows in Kansas City and Lawrence. She's done multiple commission projects including a solo show at the Great Plains Nature Center, painted two large outdoor murals and worked on children's book illustrations. Bobbie has painted murals in Ark City KS, Lawrence KS, Wichita KS, Anthony KS, and Kiowa KS. She is currently working on illustrating three books, one tattoo design, and one commission painting for a private residence.

CONTRIBUTING AUTHORS

Alisha Diane Ashley-Galloway
Anna Bartkoski
Lindsey Bartlett
Annette Hope Billings
Julie Ann Baker Brin
Chad V. Broughman
Jalia Bruce
Patricia Cleveland
Brian Daldorph
Chris "Diaz"
Thaddeus Dugan
Heather Duras
Gretchen Cassel Eick
Amber Fraley
Beth Gulley
George Gurley
David Hann
LeAhana Hunt
Debra Irsik
Kelly W. Johnston
Kathleen Kaska

Leonard Krishtalka
Edward Lee
Laura Lewis
Joseph McGovern
Ronda Miller
Samantha Moon
LaDeana Mullinix
Dan Nagengast
Peg Nichols
Kevin Rabas
Troy Robinson
Mark Scheel
Tyler Sheldon
Diana Silver
Tracy Million Simmons
Patrick Sumner
Craig Sweets
Chuck Warner
Brenda White
Heather Duras

Contents

INTRODUCTION

The ostrich is the largest bird on earth; she can weigh as much as 350 pounds. Unable to fly, an ostrich can bat her long-lashed eyes at you before she runs away at speeds of up to 70 mph. If she is unable to outrun her preditor, she'll bury her head in the sand when she's frightened, leaving only her long legs and feathered rear protruding, prefering not to view any danger coming her way. We all know this. We've seen the pictures. *Right*?

Wrong. She only sticks her nose in the sand to turn over her eggs. Ostriches do NOT stuff their faces into the earth due to fear. *Au contraire!* When frightened, the ostrich throws herself onto the ground and freezes—attempting to blend in with her surroundings.

This may be *a writers* natural response to fear, too, especially the rampant fear of words in our communities today. Just lay down and blend in.

The Playful inspires — moves us to relate;
but the perilous compels, it is why we create.

Ostriches look playful, but if you get up close to one you are definitely in peril. Cheetahs, lions, tigers, and hyennas hunt them. Writers are hunted by censors.

Censoring authors and banning books are hot topics this summer of 2023. And although it is contrary to American values—and the 1st Amendment—there may be a slight upside. Banning books makes them sexy!

Banning books was a great way to interest me and my teenage friends in reading. Tell us we weren't allowed to read something, and one of our gang would come up with a boot-legged copy for us curious middle-schoolers to peruse. We'd scour it for any tidbit. It was usually hard to figure out why the work had been banned, and we were often disappointed. We felt a sense of elation—satisfaction even—with every cuss word or spicy description we discovered.

When we entered high school, Mr. Feldman assigned *Catcher in the Rye*—we knew *that* book was *questionable*. We'd heard the talk. It was banned in other places.

I can remember the gleam in Mr. Feldman's eye as he collected the book reports from each student at quarter's end. We'd all read it. Even those who didn't like books found a few minutes away from basketball practice or TV to read about Holden Caulfield's anxious life. We read the book cuss word to cuss word, but in between, the story resonated and stuck, and it did just what Mr. Feldman expected—it made us life-long readers. Or at least some of us. And not because of the cuss words, they were just seasoning, powdered sugar.

When we read *Catcher in the Rye* or *The Outsiders* we learned more than whatever message the author was trying to convey. By reading and discussing the book, including talking about why some folks wanted it banned, we students learned about intollerance of ideas.

Banning books is again fashionable; it is all the rage today. The angry voices of those who want to limit words are loud. But there are people advocating for freedom to read, write, and share words, even if their voices are hard to hear over the din of those who fear words. It was heartening to see the spotlight on the issue of book banning at the American Library Association conference in Chicago, June 2023. Mild-mannered librarians are a fierce lot when challenged.

Sharing ideas that some might not like can be perilous, even if the writer is mindful and respectful. Children's book author Judy Bloom spoke at the ALA conference this year. She personally felt the ire of those who wish to limit speech. Her book was removed from libraries because *Are You There God, It's Me Margaret* included some language about puberty.

Jacqueline Woodson, author of *Brown Girl Dreaming* was interviewed by Late NIght's Seth Meyers. She told him "I didn't even know I was challenged or censored, I got a call from Judy Blume..."

Meyers responded, "Let me just say, as far as name-dropping goes, that's as good as it gets."

Woodson, laughing, continued, "She was doing an anthology called *Places I Never Meant to Be*, and she asked me to be in it, because it was an anthology for censored writers. And I'm like, 'I've never been censored,' and she was like, 'Oh, yes, you have.'"

> *"You read me banned books?"*
> *I say this sarcastically because I*
> *know he's making it up.*
>
> *"Almost exclusively," he answers—*
> *dead serious. "Charlotte's Web*
> *and the poetry book by—*

uh—Silverstein—uh."

"Where the Sidewalk Ends?" I say.

"And Reynolds—brave ... uh ..."

"As Brave as You? No!
How could anyone ban that?"

—Amy Sarig King, Attack of the Black Rectangles

The pressure to limit speech and avoid topics weighs heavily on authors. Writing is fraught with peril on every side. With all of the uproar about words and ideas, an author may be tempted to freeze — to try to blend in with her surroundings. The author who persists in writing her truth in spite of the potential hazard takes perilous action. And to those brave authors we offer our thanks, including and especially to Annette Hope Billings, featured in *Interview With An Author* on page 11 —"For me writing is about authenticity, truth, justice—about what's just."

Our world is filled with unwanted truths some don't want to hear; it is littered with stereotypes and slanders we must strive to overcome, and the writer who can rise above limitations to bridge gaps using words and ideas helps us all find understanding.

The Write Bridge provides a forum for authors to explore opposing ideas—seriously or in fun—to move beyond boundaries, to bridge the gap. The following articles, poems, stories and plays demonstrate the power of words to change minds and hearts, or just produce a belly-laugh. They portray the foolishness of the fear of ideas. They show how our combined knowledge and compassion can save us from our natural inclination to just lay down and freeze.

"A word to the unwise.
Torch every book.
Char every page.
Burn every word to ash.
Ideas are incombustible.
And therein lies your real fear."

—Ellen Hopkins"

In this edition of *The Write Bridge*, authors explore the topics *PERILOUS* and *PLAYFUL*, offering lessons and comic relief on our human shortcomings and aspirations.

If you enjoy reading of peril, consider "Servant of the State" by Brian Daldorph or Chad V. Broughman's enclosed story, "Ice." If you prefer humor check out "Hot, Hot, Yoga" by Amber Fraley and "Barry and the Deer" by David Hann. Or enjoy both the perilous and the playful in "A Letter From Hell" by Leonard Krishtalka or "Sloan Takes a Holiday" by Alisha Galloway.

Although descended from a flying bird, the ostrich somehow forgot how to fly. Let the writer and reader not forget how to enjoy our playful imaginings, even as we encounter the perilous.

Don't blend in. Let your writing reflect your truth. Let your reading expand your horizons. Stretch your limits, and share words that inspire.

—Maureen (Micki) Carroll, Editor-in-chief

Etymology

*The featured word for this issue's
etymology review is:*

PERILOUS

From Peril: Old French, and earlier from Latin
per - **"attempt"**
periculum **"experiment, danger,"**
"trying out of something,"
—**root of** *experiment, expert, repertory*:
"a list of things 'found,'" and Pirate
**"Someone who makes an 'attempt' or 'attack'
on someone."**

Perilously
"In a manner involving peril; very dangerously."

The quality or character of being perilous;
DANGEROUSNESS;
"The perilousness of this present time."
—*1727, Bailey Vol. II*

Fraught With Peril, Great Danger,
Full Of Risk, Hazardous

"The most arduous and perilous duties of friendship,"
—*1849, Macaulay.*

Definitions from the *Compact Edition of the Oxford English Dictionary*,
Oxford University Press 1971, and *Dictionary of Word Origins*, **John Ayto**,
Arcade Publishing 1990.

BOBBIE LYN POWELL

PART I—
ARTICLES & ESSAYS

WEAVING IT ALL TOGETHER

Featured articles submitted for the SUMMER 2023 edition of *The Write Bridge* range from the humorous to the painful. Can you take the heat? Find out in Amber Fraley's "Hot, Hot Yoga" and Dan Nagengast's "Hailstormes." What lessons have tough times taught you? Discover wisdom passed down through generations in "1918" by Laura Lewis and "Lives on the Line" by Mark Scheel. Feel the freedom of flying un-tethered in Deb Irsik's "Christmas Break," and a recognition of our limits even as we stretch them in Tracy Million Simmon's "So Cool It Hurts A Little." Remember your childish imagination in Troy Robinson's "The Kingdom of Troy" and your respect for Earth's other creatures in Chuck Warner's "What's Your Take On Snakes" and our featured essay, David Hann's "Barry and the Deer." Enjoy!

ANNETTE HOPE BILLINGS

Interview With An Author

ANNETTE HOPE BILLINGS,
AUTHOR AND POET
— by Amber Fraley

AF: Poetry has been your main choice to express yourself. Are there other forms of writing you like to express yourself with?

AHB: I also love to write short fiction, short stories, and I've written a couple of one-act plays. But poetry is my bread and butter.

AF: Who are some of your influences?

AHB: Maya Angelou, of course. Nikki Giovanni—a myriad of authors.

AF: Is there anything special about your writing space or process that you think helps you?

AHB: It may sound odd, but I think artists see the world and move through the world differently. I feel the actual writing of the poetry—whether it's by hand or on my keyboard—is the last step in the process. I think I live poetically. I see things from a poet's point of view. One of the things I love about poetry is it says volumes in a minimum amount of words. It takes out the fluff and leaves the meat. I can be in conversation with someone and hear them say a sentence and think, "Oh, man. That's a poem. That's an idea." It's not like I'm purposely listening for it. It's the way I hear it.

I'd like to say I have some very disciplined approach to writing, but that wouldn't be true. (Laughs.) But

I do try to notice things—people, sounds, words, throughout my day no matter what I'm doing, that are possible fodder for poetry. If someone asked if I write every day, I would say no. But am I poetic every day? I would say yes.

AF: What is something surprising you learned about yourself through the writing process?

AHB: I think I've been surprised by how honest I've been willing to be in my writing. As many lives do, my life contains some tragedy and trauma, and I've been surprised about how open I've been able to be over time. It's been a surprise to me to be able to be so vulnerable and still feel safe.

AF: Do you hide any secrets in your books (or poems) that only a few people will find?

AHB: I think of myself as a pretty straightforward writer that you wouldn't need to have a background story to understand it. And the other thing I've grown to know is it's okay to trust the reader to read my poetry through their own lens. I used to worry about writing in such a way that the reader would understand what happened. Well, no, that's not my job. I actually want the reader to experience it in their own way. If I read a poem that resonates to me, I'll remember that and it becomes part of my fabric. So I don't want to try to limit readers and make them see or feel a certain way.

AF: Do you view writing as a kind of spiritual practice?

Very much so. For me writing is about authenticity, truth, justice—about what's just. It's certainly part of my spirituality.

When I began writing decades ago, I was writing for my own soul healing and the thought of sharing it with the world wasn't what my goal was. But as I healed, and my writing took on a different color, and I wanted to share and have feedback, I particularly wanted to put words out there that maybe other people couldn't express. I thought part of my duty as a survivor was to help others who were still being tossed about by life. Writing about hard things is a duty.

One of my personal philosophies is art—possibly only art—can save us. I think art pulls something from an authentic place. Oftentimes people will read something, or look at a painting or sculpture, in a more accepting way than if someone just said it to them in conversation. Art provides more liberty for considering something that you might not otherwise.

It's most important that my writing create change. Can I change the world? No. Can I change a tiny increment of it in that moment? Yes.

AF: Are you originally from Kansas?

AHB: My mother was originally from the Tennessee/Kentucky area and my dad was in the army so we moved quite a bit, but wound up here in Topeka because her family was here.

AF: Do you want each poem to stand on its own, or are you trying to build a body of work with connections between each creation?

AHB: I would have to say that I like the thought of each poem having its own place. If it turns out that it's similar to, or in the company of other like poems that's wonderful, but I don't think I write with the intent of it being about a certain subject.

AF: To connect with readers, do you think a writer needs to feel emotions strongly?

AHB: I can't imagine writing from any place that isn't emotional. For me, my writing definitely comes from an emotional place and that's what helps me. Strong emotion.

AF: If you could talk to your younger writing self, what advice would you give?

AHB: I think I would tell that younger self to remember that you are a unique writer. No one else can occupy your particular place. It's okay to be in whatever stage of writing you're in. I would reassure her.

AF: Do you have relationships with other authors? How do you support each other?

AHB: Yes, I do. One of the things we do is our monthly open mic, which I'm one of the facilitators for. We support each other by attending each other's events, by buying each other's work, commenting on each other's work in gentle, supportive ways, commiserating and sharing our feelings about writing. Talking about writing can be so supportive.

(The Speakeasy Open Mic takes place the first Wednesday of every month at the ArtsConnect gallery in the NOTO district of Topeka, 909 N Kansas Ave.)

AF: Do you have any recommendations for young or aspiring writers/poets?

AHB: Develop a community of writers. Attend events that are writer oriented. Read, read, read. Consider reading genres you may not be interested in. Sometimes we don't know what we're interested in because we haven't read it yet. Find writers that speak to you and do some conscious thinking about what it is about their writing that speaks to you.

Annette Hope Billings is an award-winning poet known for the impact of her audible presentations of work. In 2015 she brought her registered nursing career to an early end to fully pursue her passion for writing. That same year her first collection of poetry, A Net Full of Hope, received Topeka's ARTSConnect's ARTY Award in Literature. Her second and third books, Descants for a Daughter and Just Shy of Stars followed. Billings' work, including prose and short stories, can also be found in a variety of anthologies as well as in print and online journals.

One of the events she values most is the monthly open mic in its tenth year, First Wednesday Speak Easy Poets Topeka, KS, which she co-hosts with fellow poet Sue Edgerton-Johnston.

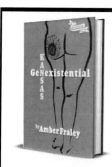

CROWNS

DIRECTED BY ANNETTE HOPE BILLINGS
Performance Date: 09/23/2023 , 7:30 pm
Theatre Lawrence
4660 Bauer Farm Dr, Lawrence, Kan., (785) 843-7469
Tickets On Sale Now!

Adapted by Regina Taylor from a book of the same name, *CROWNS* is a moving and celebratory musical in which hats become a springboard for an exploration of black history and identity. Weaving together faith, fashion and family, *CROWNS* traces the tradition of hats back to African rituals and forward to current fashion. Filled with gospel music and a little rap, the show pulses with energy and was hailed by the New York Times as "a show that seems to arise out of spontaneous combustion..."

JOSEPH MAINO, PHOTO

Hot, Hot Yoga:
Amber Fraley

For a time in the early 2000s I ran a liberal monthly rag in my hometown in Lawrence. Despite being filled with local reporting, provocative opinions, poetry, art and music, it was spectacularly unsuccessful at making money. Despite the local liberal rabble-rousers' vocal insistence they very much wanted a "progressive" alternative to the local conservative daily, they didn't seem to have much cash to pay for it. Then again, perhaps the fault was mine, and I didn't give the people what they wanted, so to speak, though I felt pulled in a thousand different directions all the time. In addition to being hardworking and earnest, our progressive community here didn't want to settle for less, and they demanded more and more coverage and more pages we couldn't really afford to provide.

Still, it was a valuable experience—I learned my sensibilities are almost all Liberal Arts and almost no Business, which is a bad combination for a publisher. I also learned I was a coward when it came to certain things — selling ads, for instance, which is the bread-and-butter of any news outlet. Writing news stories that irked the local establishment? No problem. Trying to be a real businesswoman? Somehow, I didn't have the stomach for it.

The publication did, however, have a core base of advertisers we appreciated very much. One of those advertisers was a hot yoga studio, run by one of those people whose life seems to revolve around exercise, which is fine. It's just not a lifestyle I particularly want to delve into. I *do* exercise, but there are a limited number of hours I'm willing to dedicate to get the benefits of feeling and looking better. In other words, I'm willing to be a little bit pillowy in exchange for not working out too hard for too long, but still feeling miles better than when I don't exercise at all.

The owner of the hot yoga studio was, to me, an intimidating woman. One of those exercise apostles who's determined to convert every slothful potato in her vicinity. I liked it when she mailed her checks in. I always braced myself when she wanted a face-to-face meeting about an advertising campaign.

"You should come exercise with us!" She'd say this with an air of confident enthusiasm bordering on the maniacal. She was wiry and tan, with short, silver hair, and a personality somewhere between yogi and drill sergeant. Her waist was the size of my upper thigh, and she could've kicked my ass ten times over without even mussing her hair.

Had it been any other yoga studio, I would've been thrilled to attend. I love yoga. But this was hot yoga, and I have never had a good relationship with the summer sun or the heat — even as a child — which is a shame, because I live in Kansas. It doesn't take much for me to become overheated and then dehydrated because, like my entire sweaty family on both sides, we schpritz like fountains with the least amount of effort, and the hotter it is the more we sweat. Even a short stint of gardening or walking the dog in the heat leaves me drained and with a headache that pounds away into the next day. If I don't have enough water with me to replace the deluge leaving my body, I risk passing out. It's mostly my head that sweats— yes, the whole head and face—so my hair is frequently wet in summer, and it may not be because I just got out of the shower. Frankly, it's disgusting.

But I knew I couldn't put this lady off forever. She was expecting a reciprocal business arrangement, and I also got the feeling she considered my buxomness to be a problem that needed fixing, but who knows, maybe those were my own insecurities.

One day, she cornered me. "You're coming to yoga this week," she said, arms crossed. "No excuses. We have everything here you need. You can use one of our mats. Just bring a towel, some water and yourself." It was an order. Not a request.

It just so happened that this was right at the time the yoga studio was hosting the hot yoga champion of the world. Yes, there is a hot-yoga world-champion. In order to be hot yoga champion of the world, one must transform one's body into a Davinci-like specimen of perfection. This year's world-champion of hot yoga was no exception. He was a tiny god with taut, smooth brown skin over muscle and bone. He was my height, young and Hollywood-level good-looking with a dark man-bun. He seemed to live most of his life nearly naked and shoeless in a man bikini, because yoga was his entire existence. He was the whole reason I'd been forced to show up to the yoga studio in the first place — to take photographs

JOSEPH MAINO, PHOTOGRAPHER

of his body in impossible poses no real human being could ever get into. He had the sort of body that made you want to apologize for your own. In one pose, called firefly, he held his body weight with his hands, his legs in a V around his arms, his toes pointed straight up toward the ceiling, his perfect butt several inches off the floor. I gaped in amazement as he held the pose, and he admonished me to hurry up and take the photos.

The tiny god joined the conversation, his gorgeous eyes sparkling. "Yeah, you should come this Friday! It'll be great!" I was trapped. Trapped by the tiny god and the drill sergeant. At that point, what can you do?

I smiled and nodded my head. "Okay," I heard myself say, and I knew as soon as the words came out I would stand by them no matter what.

No matter what.

But at what cost? I wondered over the next few days. Maybe it would be fine. Maybe, somehow, my lifelong battle with heat would abate itself and I would come through the experience with that sort of movie win every person deserves to have at least once in their life. Would I be able to do all the yoga poses perfectly? Obviously not, but I'd give it a damn good go, and everyone would be impressed with the fat girl who didn't completely embarrass herself at the hot yoga class. Somehow, someway, everything would work out and the day would be saved.

When I arrived for my class, I first grabbed one of their mats, which were stacked outside the yoga studio, and noted it was unusual — padded and coated in slick plastic with no slip-resistant texture to it whatsoever. It was an omen I chose to ignore.

Upon entering the studio, I was shocked and dismayed to learn the tiny god was not only in attendance, he was right up front in his tiny yogic underwear, facing us, where he'd be teaching the class. Behind him the wall was mirrored, kindly giving the room a clear view of his muscular bottom. The room was small. Two space heaters blazed away in the corners on the far wall. The floor was covered in utility carpet that looked clean, but smelled of damp sweat. The small room filled quickly and we were packed in close together. I put my hot pink mat down on the floor, claiming a spot on the edge of the room, a desperate but futile attempt to hide. I was dismayed to note every single person in the class had one specific body type: thin and muscular. Not one body deviated from this type save for mine. The mustered-up confidence I'd managed to conjure began to plummet.

This should have been a clear signal for me to listen to the little voice in my head screaming get the heck out of here! For the love of God just walk out, get in your car and drive home. No. Instead, I held my head high. I can do this I lied to myself, all the while knowing I was lying to myself. (Life hack! When you find yourself lying to yourself, for the love of all that is holy LISTEN TO YOUR LITTLE VOICE. This is how people succumb to serial killers.)

Then the tiny god walked to the back of the tiny boxlike room with the sweaty carpet and shut the door.

The temperature in the room shot up from eighty or so degrees to the Bikram Yoga-approved purgatory of one-hundred-and-five-degrees Fahrenheit. I started with the class, attempting the poses as well as I could, despite the fact I'd only dabbled in yoga before. At the time, I didn't really understand the broad range of difficulty in various yoga disciplines that range from restorative to meditative to punish-your-body-into-perfection yoga. This was clearly the latter and I had no business being there.

A few minutes into the class I realized why the yoga mats were the way they were — smooth so that sweat could be wiped off. The waterfall of sweat I knew would eventually come pouring off my head came soon enough, and there was nothing I could do to stop it. My face blazed red but I didn't need to see it in the mirror because I could feel it, the heat collecting in my forehead as though someone had an iron pressed to it. Between every pose I gulped at my bottle of water that was laughably small. I began to melt on the yoga pad like a pat of butter on a griddle, sliding around in my own sweat, which puddled under my knees and elbows or hands or feet, depending on which body parts were making depressions in the padded mat.

I can't remember now how many minutes into the class before I collapsed on my mat and lie there a few moments, trying to catch my breath, praying to recover an ounce of the strength that was rapidly leaving my body. After allowing me to lie there in peace for a few seconds, the tiny god addressed me:

"Can't you get up at all?" A titter went through the class.

"No," I replied, and they laughed. Normally I would be mortified, but at that point I was so far into heat exhaustion I wasn't even offended. I was just trying to stay conscious and not slip into heat stroke. I couldn't be mad at the ultra-fit skinny people. I could only be mad at myself — I'd known how this was going to go from the outset, but I'd done it anyway. After a couple minutes I struggled to my hands and knees, but collapsed again into my puddle of warm body fluid, knowing I wouldn't be able to hold another pose both because my body was shutting down and because I was slipping around so badly. The sultry heat of moist bodies and lights and space heaters was inescapable. Yes, even the perfect body people sweated, though it was more of a sports commercial sort of glisten. Somehow I muddled my way through the rest of the class, though I don't remember much. As soon as the tiny god ended the class and opened the door I bolted, drove home, vomited, went to bed and slept for twelve solid hours.

I thought I'd escaped, but a few days later the phone rang. It was the silver-haired drill sergeant.

"I expect to see you in class next week." she said. I knew I couldn't go back.

"I threw up and slept for twelve hours," I replied.

"That's what your body needed." She sounded one-hundred-percent positive. I knew she had no idea what she was talking about, because she had no idea what it was like to live inside my body, just as I had no idea what it was like to live inside hers. (Fabulous, I should imagine.)

"I don't do well in the heat," I said, knowing she wouldn't hear me.

"That heat is natural. It is a hundred and five degrees in India where yoga originated. It's what the body needs to exercise properly."

"Okay," I said, and ended the call.

I waited a couple days to call back, praying for her voicemail to pick up. It did.

"I'm not coming back to class. I'm sorry, I just can't." I hung up before she could pick up the call and catch me. I could imagine her on the other end, listening to my message, shaking her head in disapproval.

The hot yoga studio stayed a loyal customer until our newspaper went out of business a few months later. The studio managed to stay in business for many years.

Many years later, I'd go back to yoga. Regular temperature yoga. The teacher was a friend, and like me, middle-aged. Also like me, her body was not perfect, but yoga made her nimble and flexible and strong, and she became my shero. Her class was challenging, but she was willing to make modifications for injuries or even just stiff joints. Her classes were made up of young people and old people of varying body types, and she helped us all adjust our routine to fit our own needs and fitness levels. There was never a feeling of competition.

Still, even though My yoga instructor and I had been friends for some time, she'd never really seen me sweat. No one ever quite believes me when I try to describe it. It's something that must be seen to be believed. Even in her air-conditioned studio with an industrial-sized ceiling fan circulating, after just a few yoga moves the sweat would begin to flow down my face, my wet hands slipping on my non-slip yoga mat. In addition to a large bottle of water, I'd try to remember to bring a bandanna to wipe off sweat between poses.

"You sweat a lot," she observed one day in class.

Believe me, sister. I know.

Amber Fraley, author of *Kansas GenExistential* and *The Bug Diary*, is your typical Gen Xer Kansas wife and mom of one who grew up a book nerd in a dysfunctional family and now writes about those experiences as hilarious therapy. She's the author of *From Kansas, Not Dorothy*, and the viral essay "**Gen X Will Not Go Quietly**," as well as numerous human interest articles. Amber loves Kansas, is frequently awkward in public, and desperately wishes to see a tornado and live to tell the tale.

KANSAS GENEXISTENTIAL | AMBER FRALEY
ISBN-13: 978-1-960462-13-8
Publication Date: 12/6/2023 | 6 X 9; 130 pages; $21.99

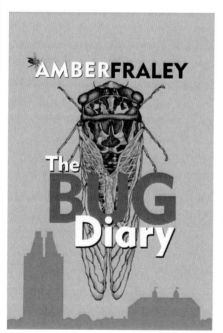

So Cool
It Hurts A Little:
Tracy Million Simmons

You must be the cool aunt," the man says as Keira and I get out of the car at the skating rink. Until that moment, I was undecided about roller skating. I loved to roller skate as a kid and enjoyed skating with my own kids when they were young, but when my 7-year-old great-niece asked if I would skate with her, my 52-year-old brain summoned up a long pause before answering . . "I might just watch."

But how could I not skate now that this stranger, a man twenty years my junior, has called me cool?

The kid at the ticket window is surprised when I say I plan to skate too. "You don't have to pay if you are just watching."

"I'm skating," I answer. The decision is made, and Keira's grin is the exclamation point on the decision.

I sign the release of liability form, and my internal monologue tells my cautious brain, which is continuing to sound an alarm, to shut up. It's my older sister who usually gets the "fun aunt" label, and I can't remember the last time my sister agreed to put on roller skates.

The psychedelic carpet, the lighting, the sound of wheels on that blue painted concrete floor . . . it all brings the joy of skating rushing back to me as I pull on over-worn boots with classic orange rubber wheels and extra-long ratty laces that I have to pull and pull to "snug" my narrow feet into that wide space further stretched by the thousands of feet that must have come before mine.

After a few rounds of the rink, I am semi-graceful. Sure, my knees ache, and my ankles throb, but I am skating, by golly, and I am having a mighty fine time.

An hour in, I am confident enough to risk a turn, and I find myself skating, no, gliding backward. Hello, days of yore!

My niece lights up when she sees me and pilots a few rounds by holding my hands, making sure no one is behind me. We make our way to the center of the rink and link arms, feet in ballet position two, pulling together to spin in a tight circle. My mind returns to the faces of my buddies of the fifth grade, the sixth grade, the seventh grade—skating in the era before it became a guilty pleasure, peer-pressured by my "cool" friends off the calendar of events.

My niece does the limbo, and I ache to join her, but I surreptitiously squat once and end up on my butt, my prowess on skates less well-defined than my memory of it. I'll practice, I tell myself. How low I will go once again. I just need to spend some time working on it. I mentally add skating rink hours to my to-do list.

An hour and forty-five minutes in and I'm feeling good about my decision to go roller skating. I may be 52 years

JOSEPH MAINO, PHOTO

old, but I'm a young 52, an active, strong, and destined-for-an-old-age-of-adventure-52. What felt like a perilous activity a short time ago, now presents a welcome challenge.

It's about that time that a child in front of me stumbles. My mind turns the whole thing into a slow-motion movie reel as I imagine my young-skater-self flipping her skates sideways, circling the crash site without a glitch, and then stopping to help the child back to his feet.

My 52-year-old body, however, responds to the voice inside my head that is shrieking, *Oh gawd, please don't fall! This is going to hurt!*

As the child crashes, spread-eagle forward, I topple backward, effectively stopping myself from running the kid over and causing real damage to his tiny body. He's young and flexible. He's got years of bounce ahead.

"At least you didn't hurt the boy," my niece says later, helping me find the bright side, true to our family's form.

But the look on that poor child's face when he sees me is damage enough. True terror lights his eyes as he rights himself, looking at me on the floor next to him. "Are you OK?" he asks breathlessly, his concern for the pain he must witness on my face apparent.

"I will be," I answer, determined not to let him see me cry.

A late-night trip to the ER reveals the first diagnosed broken bone of my life, a small bone in the center of my wrist.

"It's very common in an extreme sprain, the ER doc says. He demonstrates the tendon's location, and says it sometimes takes a little piece of bone with it upon impact. I leave the ER hours later with an elbow to fingertip splint on my left arm and instructions for managing the pain. Three days later, the orthopedic specialist I visit declares it non-surgical. Six weeks in a brace—a plaster cast remains an option if the pain is too great—and three months before I will feel my hand strength has returned to normal.

No. Big. Deal.

For the first week, I pop pain pills like candy and mourn the loss of my return-to-skating plans. In flashes, I find myself contemplating a skating rehab program. With improved balance, a gain in strength and flexibility, and perhaps with some roller skates that custom-fit my feet, I could still do this. I strategize the training schedule for longer than seems healthy. I could become a roller-skating diva before I'm 60, perhaps join a roller derby team.

But at what cost? A more reasoned voice inside my head asks. The inability to type with two hands has completely destroyed the pace of my professional life as a writer and publisher. It's frustrating, yet at times it feels like a much-needed shift in perspective. When one's speed is forcibly changed, one limb rendered useless, the brain rewires, building new circuitry to accommodate. Within those pauses, allowing time for these changes, I have moments of clarity, as if the lessons from what may be the last perilous but playful skating activity of mine will have lasting repercussions, and not all of the bad kind.

There are many ways to be cool, after all, and some of those things involve activities other than strapping wheels to my feet.

Tracy Million Simmons enjoys reading and writing about the people and places of her home state of Kansas, both real and imagined. She is the owner of Meadowlark Press, based in Emporia, Kansas, which publishes books of poetry, fiction, and non-fiction. Tracy is the author of *Tiger Hunting,* a novel (Chasing Tigers Press, 2013) and *A Life in Progress,* short stories (CTP/Meadowlark, 2017).

Hailstorms, Tornadoes, Dust Storms & Blizzards:

Dan Nagengast

Hailstorms

One summer day, my father was a few miles from our home, cultivating our summer-fallowed fields with a rod-weeder pulled behind a D4 Caterpillar. A black cloud grew all afternoon in the West, and finally it reached him. Big splats of rain hit him and the Caterpillar, and then he saw the first baseball-sized hail stones whizz in at an angle. He shut down immediately, and crawled under the Cat.

A D4 was a relatively small Cat, but it still weighed about 10,000 pounds, 3 times that of a car. It is basically a mobile hunk of heavy iron. There was no cab, and the one safe place for my father, for many miles around, was under the tractor. A few surely hit the Cat, but I rode that tank for countless hours later, over many summers, and there was not a hailstone ding to be seen. They don't make them like that anymore.

Dad brought home a few hailstones for mom and we kids to admire. My hometown, Potter, Nebraska, long held the record for the largest hailstone ever recorded in the world. The storm that produced it hit the afternoon of July 6, 1928. The hailstones were generally as large as grapefruit and weighed up to a pound and a half. This is from a Weather Bureau Office report:

No particular damage was done by this record-breaking hail, except a few roofs were slightly injured, four houses and a garage reporting holes torn through the roof by the gigantic

(c)JMaino

but widely scattered hailstones. We would estimate that about 10 stones fell on each space the size of an ordinary town lot. They fell from 10 to 15 feet apart. The monster chunks of ice could be heard hissing through the air, and when they hit in plowed or soft ground completely buried themselves, and sank halfway in on prairie ground. In a letter confirming this statement Mr. Stevens gave the following additional description of the appearance of these stones: The stones, most of which measured around 14 inches in circumference, were smooth, of clear ice, and made up of concentric rings around a single center. Some stones were jagged, having the appearance of one large stone with a number of little stones frozen on its outside.

Okay, the sound of grapefruit-sized hailstones, hissing through the air and burying themselves in the ground kind of freaks me out a bit. The largest one measured was 17" in diameter. One stone found was broken, but of concentric circles inside. If whole, it was estimated it would have been the size of a human head.

The Great Plains are not the only hail-prone areas of the world. Some of the most damaging storms, in terms of livestock and wildlife and human death have occurred in India and Australia.

These prairies I grew up on, were inhabited for thousands of years before the white people came. The Arapaho lived semi-nomadic lives in Western Nebraska. They lived in tepees and moved with the aid of dog *travois*. The Pawnee lived to the east and had permanent, earth-covered structures there, which surely offered protection, but when on the hunt, they used tepees. It seems like those hide-covered portable houses would also offer protection, but, like my father, people would often find themselves far from home when the skies went on a killing spree. And before the Arapaho and Pawnee, there were just the buffalo and the antelope.

What a terror those storms must have been to herds of wildlife.

I experienced some heavier hail storms that completely wiped out crop fields, stripped every leaf from the trees and reducing woodies to bare, broken sticks protruding from the ground. It brought an eerie, brown winter landscape in the midst of high summer, with wheat fields muddled into the taupe earth, where minutes before rolled a brilliant dark green, 2-foot tall waving sea of promise. Birds are gone. Insects are gone. It is heart breaking.

Tornadoes

Tornadoes, during the daylight hours, were things to be watched for, to be watched closely when sighted, and to scurry away and hide from if you couldn't get an eye on them. So, if things blew up in the dark of night, you went to the storm cellar to hide.

Our house had a basement, about 6' down, with small windows at shoulder level to allow in the light. Below that level, we had a storm shelter, maybe 12 to 14 feet below ground level. It had steep concrete stairs with 14" risers, which were really hard to negotiate for we small children -like a series of ledges we had to be helped down. There was a single light bulb dangling high above. My mother had rough wooden shelves down there, where she kept her home-canned goods, mostly plums, pears and peaches, but also some canned green beans, tomatoes and sauce.

We waited out many storms there at night in the dark and cobwebs. Sometimes for a few minutes, but others for an hour or two, huddled down in the earth till things seemed clear.

During the day, you went out and watched the clouds and the storm. On the prairie, you could see for miles, and watch storms build and dissipate. You could generally tell if they would pass by, or if they had a bead on you. Folklore had it that tornado-bearing storms would have a greenish tinge to them. Folklore said they always come from the Southwest and head Northeast. Folklore says some places are protected from tornadoes by topography.

I recall one summer day, riding the Caterpillar, watching three separate tornadoes at the same time. All were miles away in three different cells, none of them headed my direction. I worked on.

Tornadoes are devastating when they hit congested areas, but in Western Nebraska, the targets were sparse. I do recall being packed into the car to go look at two different farms that got hit.

Catastrophe sight-seeing. One place lost a barn and had a combine flipped. Their cattle were still missing. The other place was just a few miles south of us, and the storm had come in the night while the couple was sleeping. They were awakened by the impact of a massive shard from their mirror embedded and vibrating in their head board between them. They were unscratched with the roof gone and the howling sky above them.

Over the course of time though, many farmsteads have suffered some damage. I came to realize that because of the tire nails my first car picked up, often miles from farmsteads or places where spent nails should be. Buildings destroyed leaving scattered nails for miles.

Again, I wonder what tornadoes seemed like to the first people.

Dust Storms

Dust storms were a summertime phenomenon. A combination of meteorology and landscape conditions. Large fronts coming in often carried rain, but sometimes they would be dry. There would be a huge burst of wind over miles of dry summer fallowed fields. If so, a dust cloud built, and they were awesomely ominous as they approached.

We had one parcel of land a few miles east of our house, that was forever marked by the dust bowl years. The mile long straight line, running north/south between two field strips was clearly a foot and a half lower on one side than the other. The lower east side had been fallow one summer in the '30s, and all that soil blew away to Appalachia.

Dust storms were brown in Western Nebraska. You could see them coming for miles, but it was difficult to judge their speed. They roiled. They looked like trouble, and they got to you a lot sooner than you thought they would.

I got caught on the little tractor once. I had been over to our east fields with a little Minneapolis Moline tricycle tractor (two small wheels close together for steering on the front, with the large traction tires on the back.) My dad and I had been moving equipment out of the quonset hut, where we kept the bailer, the combine, and other pieces of machinery that were only occasionally used. The little tractor had rubber tires and could go in on the concrete and pull stuff out. We were probably getting the combine out to prep it for harvest.

Anyway, late in the day I was headed home. The seat was up high on that tractor, again, with no cab. I could see the storm coming and there was no place to go so I continued toward home and headed straight into the storm. It was blinding when it hit, and I had to squint to keep my eyes open because of the dust. Visibility dropped to just the tractor around me, but I could make out the gravel ridge at the side of the road so I kept going. And I discovered a weird phenomenon. I could hold my finger out about 2 inches from the yellow Minnie fenders, and a blue spark would jump across! Fun with static electricity!

I would later be in a much worse dust storm, a haboob, in Senegal. I will write about that some other time.

It seems to me that dust storms were not something the first peoples experienced. Prairie grasses do a good job of keeping soil where it is supposed to be.

Blizzards

Snow seemed to fall sideways in Western Nebraska, always accompanied by winds, so drifts were a fact of life. The gravel roads were built up high, to blow the snow off in the winter. The barrow pits would fill with giant drifts.

Around the farm, drifts would build in the lee of buildings. Their shapes reflected wind patterns, so it helped me visualize the invisible wind.

We often had blizzards, and they could result in a day or two off from school, until the maintainer could get out and clear the roads.

Dad had a homemade bulldozer for his Cat, made by a neighbor who moonlighted as a welder and blacksmith on his farm. It was an unbelievably heavy and awkward thing, but it did the trick in keeping our lane open. Once, one of the oil fields hired dad to come with his dozer and clear out the access roads to their pumps up in the hills. He bundled up with his cap pulled down over his ears and took off. Top speed on the Cat was about 4 miles an hour so it probably took him a couple of hours just to get to where he would work. And then home again. He was gone all day. I imagine the engine's heat helped keep him warm. The money must have been a windfall of sorts for us.

People could stay home then, because they were more self-sufficient. People didn't go to town but once a week anyway. Most of our food, other than dry goods, came from the farm, or was bought in summer by the bushel, and canned. The freezer was full of beef and chicken. The cellar was full of canned fruit and vegetables. The furnace was a gravity propane type, which needed no electricity. Same with the stove and oven.

We had a big late blizzard once, maybe in May, when I was about a 5th or 6th grader. It took out the electrical lines, which caused a problem because of our freezer. Mom made us go dig a hole in the nearest snow drift, and we cleaned everything out of the freezer and put it in the drift till the power came back on.

Several times, over the years, the power went out when we had already received 150 baby chicks. They were kept in the brooder house in a large cardboard circle under a heat lamp.

Without electricity, they would have surely frozen or many of them would have suffocated as they piled together for heat. They were brought into the house in cardboard boxes and put in front of the open oven, running full blast. It was comforting to hear their peeps through the night.

The Arapaho and Pawnee could migrate, and their time spent in Western Nebraska might have been the summer, during hunting trips. I wonder whether any of them chose to remain out on the prairie during the winter.

Bison are winter-proof and walk directly into blizzards. It is thought that they are instinctively passing through the storm quicker than if they stayed still or moved in the storm's direction. In times of deep snow, they use their amazing neck muscles to move snow aside with their head to reach the grass and forage. This provides cleared pathways for pronghorn to forage afterwards.

Cattle, on the other hand, drift with the storm, and can pile up against fences or in draws where they succumb. The Big Die Up of 1886, also known as the Great Cattle Extinction was a storm and harsh winter that effectively ended the Northern Range cattle industry from Montana and the Dakotas down into Wyoming and Nebraska. The decimation of his herd in Medora, South Dakota sent Teddy Roosevelt back to the East Coast, and on to other things.

If you can't stand the heat or the cold or the dust or the hail, stay out of the Great Plains.

Dan Nagengast grew up on a farm in the Nebraska Panhandle. After small town things he eventually ended up in law school in NYC. He followed that with 8 years in villages in West Africa. He has lived in Kansas since 1984, serving as director for Church World Service, Executive Director for the Kansas Rural Center, and owner of *Seeds From Italy*, farming throughout with his wife Lynn Byczynski.

1918:
Laura Lewis

Meeting the challenge of caring for her aging father-in-law and two young sons, a young mother listens patiently to the experiences of a very young man in WWI, and discovers that she has learned something.

In 1984, Bryan, my husband's eighty-five-year-old father sat before the fireplace in his sheepskin-lined coat. Cigarette smoke swirled over his head. The plastic urinal, still capped, swayed at his knee above the puddle of pee beneath his feet.

"Hi, Sis." He greeted me as if it wasn't three o'clock in the morning. "When Mike comes today, I want to have that lawnmower ready for him."

There wasn't any lawnmower. And Mike wouldn't be coming. Mike, the other son, the favorite son, never even called, let alone came. I held my breath as the cigarette hung, trembling and forgotten, between the two, long, nicotine stained fingers draped over the arm of Bryan's chair. Ashes drifted to the floor.

"Bryan, we talked about smoking in the night. Remember? I need for you to wait until Kenny gets up at six, to make sure everything is set up for you."

"I had to use the urinal, don't you see, Sis? And I managed. Nobody has to wait on me. Let the boy sleep a little longer. He works too hard."

"But you forgot to open the cap again, Bryan." The mess had to be cleaned up, the floor- tile cloroxed and his clothing changed. Getting him set up at the kitchen bar, with his pump-pot of coffee and an ashtray, would leave me having to speed through getting the boys ready for school. Their breakfast would be a hurried one… again.

I looked at Bryan. The chin was wobbling. Tears stood in the faded eyes that had been sightless for almost two years. The puddle faded in significance. I picked up the smoldering butt from where it had dropped to the floor and rubbed it out in the ashtray.

Hitching our old five-legged piano stool over with my toe, I sat down as if the pee thing had never happened.

"Did you start smoking when you were in the Navy, Bryan?"

"What say, Sis?" he turned bleary eyes toward me as if he could see.

"Tell me about when you joined the Navy."

The chin firmed. The yellowed fingers reached for another cigarette. I gave him the pack and held the light for him.

"Well," he chuckled, "I didn't so much join the Navy as I ran away from home. I left in 1917…before the new crop of mules came for Dad to set me to breaking. He sold them to the government, you know."

And so, the story began. I had heard it before, or at least parts of it. But with every telling, it always twisted a little at my heart; to think of that boy…so long ago…who endured so much.

He told of the joyful ride from Holden, Missouri, to St. Louis to enlist, and the young girl, who sneaked out of town to flag him down and insist on going with him.

He told of the hardship he was leaving; the grim and self-serving demands of a harsh father and the bone shaking hours "breaking" mules for the sale barn at Warsaw.

He spoke of his service during that war; the one that was supposed to end all wars.

His Navy discharge papers said he was a Fireman 3rd Class. And deep in the bowels of the U.S.S. Something-or-other he had labored, stripped to the waist, shoveling coal into the great maws of the ship's furnaces to maintain the power the steam provided.

He worked alongside other men through fourteen-hour shifts. Every now and then the ship would lurch and shudder, telling the shovelers that those who worked above deck were fighting and dying behind great guns that swept the sea alongside of them, reaching for the enemy.

And they knew the enemy was reaching back.

"But they never sunk us." He spoke with pride. "They never sunk us and we kept a good head of steam."

When Influenza began to diminish their numbers he often shoveled, in one-hundred-and-twenty-degree heat, all day and into the night without ever knowing the beginning, or the ending of either. On the rare occasions he was allowed to break and seek some air top-side, he would see the bodies on deck, sewn into canvas, stacked "like cigars in a box".

He spoke of being so near home, when they were quarantined in New Orleans.

He told of how finally, when he himself fell, he had lain in his bunk for weeks, looking to die. I began thinking of how to lead the story to a good stopping place, but he found it himself.

"And I would have died for sure if it hadn't been for my Bosun. He never went down. He must have been immune. Anyway, he kept bringing me stuff to drink. Sometimes water… sometimes stuff that tasted like paint thinner. He made me drink everything he brought and I did, even when it came back up. Anyway, I didn't die."

It was good to hear him chuckle.

At some point, in the telling, there in my living room on that cool November morning, my young sons had crept out of bed and sat huddled on the couch, listening to Grampa's story.

They were late for school that day, but I like to think they learned something. I think they might have learned a little about being old, and about being young. And maybe a little of what comes in between.

Laura Lewis is a retired, farmer, mother and grandmother with a B.S. in Communications and Public Relations from Central Missouri University and an award winning writer of prose and poetry. Her work has been published in several anthologies: Kaleidoscope's *Reflections of Women's Journeys: In my Shoes*, KelLee Parr's *More Voices of the Willows*; and the *Adoption Hub of America,* short stories in two publications of "Chicken Soup for the Soul" and Wising Up Press's *Power of the Pause*. She has also self-published *Where Roses Grow,* a historical novel of the 18th century. She now resides in Kansas City, Missouri.

Subscribe to *The Write Bridge Biannual Literary Journal*

https://anamcara-press.com/
subscribe-to-the-journal/

**COMMUNITY, LOVE,
BOOKS & PUGS**

Serving readers and the
community since 2020 with
handmade coffee and pastries,
locally produced art and gifts,
and special events for
everyone.

Lives On The Line:
Mark Scheel

Adapted From A Memoir-In-Progress

My first assignment after training with the American Red Cross in 1968 was at Fort Leonard Wood, Missouri. The war in Vietnam was going full tilt then, and I knew it would only be a matter of months before I ended up deployed overseas. I was billeted at Fort Leonard Wood with some other Red Cross personnel in BOQ rooms near our office, one of the occupants there being a hospital worker named Marva. A short-haired brunette of medium build with a roundish face and a winning smile, she'd been gifted with an enviable, bubbly personality. During my tour of duty, we became friends, socializing with the group after hours, sharing some literary interests and musical preferences in common. But we lost touch after my departure to another assignment at the Great Lakes Naval Training Center near Chicago.

I arrived in Vietnam in July of 1969 and was posted to a substation at Bearcat, the Thai Panther Division area of operation. Not long after that, I discovered Marva had been deployed to a military hospital not far from my location. We reconnected once more by phone and agreed to meet again when we had mutual days off and catch up and explore some of Saigon together. So, at an opportune time for us both, I arranged with a Thai major, whom I'd befriended, to borrow his jeep and driver for the day, and the driver and I scooted over and picked up Marva and headed out under a scorching sun on the congested highway for Saigon.

Fortunately, the driver was familiar with the city and after a fashion served as a tour guide. We visited an ornate Buddhist temple and had our picture taken on the steps. Had a lunch of noodles with chicken and tea in a small street cafe, Marva musing with a laugh, "We may be playing Russian roulette with food poisoning!" (We avoided cool drinks because we'd been warned the ice was sometimes frozen from river water.) Finally, we attended a soccer match that afternoon before climbing into the jeep for the return trip to our posts. At the end of that day, however, a precarious teaching moment stood waiting in my near future.

Upon arriving at Marva's assigned hospital, she invited me to have one for the road in the officers' club before I proceeded back to my home office. I agreed and we lingered over drinks and reminisced about Fort Leonard Wood and our time there and what had transpired for us both thereafter before arriving in Vietnam. I walked her to her quarters and tarried there at the door a good while (men weren't allowed in the women's sleeping rooms) before finally taking my leave.

Returning to my driver and jeep, I was dismayed to discover the time had gotten away and the sun was about to set. The return route had cleared of traffic. The Viet Cong, of course, owned the country after dark. My driver was quite visibly alarmed, and after we departed the last checkpoint, he floored the jeep on the open road. I recalled then that an ambush had occurred the previous week near this locale. The Viet Cong were, to be sure, active hereabouts. And a lone jeep could present a prime target.

My driver then asked me did I know how to shoot a Colt .45? I told him "yes." He pleaded that I procure his weapon from its holster that rested on the floor of the jeep and prepare myself to return fire if we encountered hostilities. Knowing a .45 wouldn't be much in a firefight, still I did so to assuage his obvious concern and chambered a round, holding the pistol at the ready as we sped along while the red ball of sun sank below the dark jungle line. More than fear, a sense of guilt swept over me as I realized that through my careless indulgence I'd put another man's life at risk. I had no moral right to do that. And I vowed never to let that happen again.

The checkpoint at the main gate of Bearcat had never seemed so welcoming, and we both drew a sigh of relief as we crossed inside and headed for the motor pool. And I offered a silent gesture of gratitude to the Heavens above that we'd returned intact. But, just as importantly, I gave thanks that a vital lesson had been driven home to me which I'd carry the rest of my days. A lesson about one's obligations to the wellbeing of one's fellowman when lives may be on the line, and taught without my having had to endure the tragic consequences of neglect.

Mark Scheel grew up in east-Kansas farm country. Prior to writing full time he served with the American Red Cross, taught at Emporia State University, worked with the Johnson County Library in Shawnee Mission, Kansas, and a prose editor for *Kansas City Voices* magazine. He co-authored the *Book Of Youth and the River: the Mississippi Adventure of Raymond Kurtz, Sr.* and his collection of stories and poems, *A Backward View,* was awarded the 1998 J. Donald Coffin Memorial Book Award from the Kansas Authors Club. His blog series, *The Pebble: Life, Love, Politics and Geezer Wisdom*, was published in book form in 2015 and his fiction collection, titled *And Eve Said Yes: Seven Stories and a Novella* appeared from Waldorf Publishing in 2019.

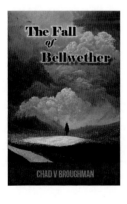

In the small town of Bellwether, where prejudice and judgment prevail, five harrowing life paths collide and a saga of survival, defiance, and unyielding human spirit unfolds.

THE FALL OF BELLWETHER
CHAD V. BROUGHMAN
ISBN-13: 978-1-960462-14-5
Publication Date: 2/29/24 | 398 pages

Double-Duty:
Peg Nichols

People who live in small communities take for granted that they will be expected to serve in more than one capacity. Other resources being scarce, their willingness is often stretched to the breaking point. Some residents of Sarcoxie, Missouri, a small town on I-44 halfway between Joplin and Springfield, serve as volunteers of an ambulance service.

Early one morning the ambulance service telephone rang in the homes of the volunteers. It was picked up by Neil Barnett, an electrical engineer by trade. After hearing a request for aid, he listened in vain for the voice of another volunteer. The guidelines of the service required a minimum of two volunteers, one to drive the ambulance without distraction, the other to attend to the needs, as far as possible, of the patient; Neil heard no other voice, only his, asking futilely if there was another volunteer on the line.

The call was not an emergency, only urgent. A Sarcoxie citizen, an elderly woman, wanted to be taken to a hospital in Joplin, twenty-five miles to the west. Sarcoxie being only a few blocks wide in any direction, Neil was soon at the ambulance barn. He kept his eyes attentive to any other resident who might be out and about despite the early hour. The streets were empty.

He was already familiar with the address; the woman had requested ambulance serviced before. By himself, he managed to get the woman into the ambulance and settled on a gurney. Still anxious to find another volunteer, Neil made one last attempt. He decided to make a turn around the town square.

In luck.

Not only was there a person on the square, it was a fellow volunteer.

Lea Schaeffer ran the only food establishment on the square, still in her night clothes to set the beans to cooking.

Neil pulled the ambulance next to Lea on the sidewalk. "I'm taking a patient to Joplin and I need another volunteer. Get in."

Lea tugged her robe closer around her shoulders. "I can't go. I'm not dressed."

"Get in," Neil ordered. "If you don't come along to help me, I'll be taking this ambulance to Joplin with two patients."

What to do when you are locked down by a heartless virus? Peg Nichols found it a perfect time to write a novel – *Sidewalk Sale Across America* – about how the Harkins try to hang on to family and livelihoods through a heartless virus. Peg Nichols is a long-time Kansas Authors Club member and member of the writing community in NE Kansas.

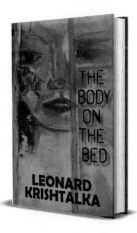

CATHY MARTIN, WATERCOLOR

Christmas Break:
Debra Irsik

Every year as Christmas break drew near, my brother and two sisters would get excited about going to the farm. When I was about fourteen, that meant going to Utica, Kansas, and spending time on my step-dad's farm. We always found adventure and relaxed rules a bit of a stimulant. We could ride horses, walk the creeks, explore silo's and find things to do that were not possible living in town.

My step-dad was a renegade himself and loved to do things with us. Sometimes we had to work a little magic on him, but he usually came through. He was a collector of junk automobiles and farm equipment. Jerry was the epitome of "Jerry-rigging." He told us stories of how he and his brothers would rig-up old auto hoods as sleds and we set our minds to doing just that.

Four or five inches of fresh snow ignited our imaginations and our desire to try the car-hood sledding. First, we helped with morning chores, which entailed hauling hay-bales out to the cows. This was always an adventure. We would pile into the truck, which had a cattle guard on the front. Jerry would slowly drive while we cut the strings on the bales. We pulled squares of hay from each bale and tossed it to the increasing number of cows crowding around the truck. We would throw it as far as we could to encourage them to move back. The truck had numerous dents; proofs that the cattle had gotten too close. The mirrors were bent at odd angles and the doors had the butt print of more than one cow. Jerry was not disinclined to bump them along with the cattle guard on the front to keep them moving.

This particular morning, my brother and I were in the back of the truck and my younger sister was riding up front. Jerry had moved away from the herd to check on a few lone critters that seemed to be uninterested in the feed. Rick and I had finished with most of the bales and were sitting on the sides of the truck bed. One of the cows was acting acted weird. She was foaming at the mouth and stumbling. When Jerry tried to get it to move, it turned and head butted the truck. No matter what angle he came from, it was obstinate, and Rick decided we could help. We jumped down and started waving our arms at the cow. She turned wild and crazy eyes on us and started running in our direction. Jerry had moved the truck up to turnaround and we were sitting ducks in the middle of a field.

Our saving grace was an old silo about twenty feet away. Rick started toward it and I was hot on his heels. We climbed the ladder on the side and the cow slammed her head against the silo. Jerry moved the truck to the bottom of the silo and we climbed into the back, but the cow slammed its head into the truck again. Jerry called out the window, "leave it. I'll see what's going on with her later. She must have got into some loco weed. Relieved, we headed back to the house. I was shaking, and not just from the cold.

I looked at my brother. "Do cows get rabies?"

He shrugged. "I don't know, but she was crazy."

After lunch, we were warm, and our hearts stopped racing. We regaled everyone with our tale of impending death and were ready to go sledding.

We talked Jerry into letting us use a couple of old car hoods and invited the cousins to sled with us. Jerry pulled one hood and Rick and an older cousin took turns driving the other truck. We were having a blast, with the trucks pulling us and zig-zagging around the field. My sister Glenny and I were behind the truck, with Jerry as our driver. The car hood was from a 1940-something car. You know the kind with the seam down the middle of it. It had a onetime sported a shiny hood ornament, but the holes were now relegated to the rope that pulled us across the pasture. Four inches of snow gave us a cushion, but there were still rocks and holes that made the ride a little rough. We bundled up until we could barely reach up and touch our own nose, which made it harder to hang on.

As luck would have it, after several passes around the pasture, swinging left and right, we ran into trouble. We were squealing and holding on for dear life. It was like skiing behind the boat with Jerry, trying everything to get us thrown off. Suddenly, the sled lurched and made a screeching sound. Glenny's half of the sled separated from mine and she went soaring away from the truck. My half of the hood remained attached to the rope. I was screaming, "Stop! It broke. Stop." Jerry slowed and watched as Glenny's sled eventually slowed and came to a stop.

We were never really in danger because it was a large open pasture, but the excitement of flying un-tethered was almost too much... almost. We collected ourselves and got in the truck with Jerry, getting warm and chattering about the adventure. We watched the other truck pulling the cousins and Rick for a couple of rounds and we waved them down to have another turn.

The next morning, Rick and I went with Jerry to check on the crazy cow. There was another one to doctor, and Jerry took care of it first. Then we drove around until we came to a grove of trees and brush. The cow was dead. Jerry hem-hawed around and I bombarded him with questions.

"Did it have rabies? Can the other cows get rabies from it? Why was it foaming at the mouth?"

Jerry shook his head and mumbled, "Locoweed. I'll have to call the dead truck." His posture indicated that was the end of it. I looked at Rick. He shrugged.

With all this excitement in the first four days of the two-week break. I could hardly wait for the next adventure.

Debra Irsik retired from the beauty industry after over twenty-five years. She is a Kansas girl and shares her life with her husband Mike, and children John and Emily. Deb is a member of The Kansas Authors Club, and Emporia Writing Group. Her Heroes by Design Y.A. fiction series was completed in 2020 and she is dedicating her time to creating a book of poetry and writing essays, prose and fiction. Deb also has published works in 105 Meadowlark Reader and The Write Bridge. She was an Amity literary prize finalist in 2023. The contest is sponsored by Anamcara Press.

MAUREEN CARROLL PHOTOGRAPHER

The Kingdom of Troy:
Troy Robinson

As I journey back through the mists of memory, a smile slowly engulfs my face, and I settle upon the most adventurous time of my life. That wondrous period between the ages of five and ten when I lived on my grandparents' farm. For a young explorer like myself, nothing compares to the exhilaration I experienced daily.

On a gradually sloping hill behind the house stood a majestic barn of white-washed wood and gray corrugated metal. The first floor was the type of dirt rife with the accumulations of ancient decay. In here my grandfather stored many fascinating objects of metal and wood.

Behind the horse-drawn medicine wagon, beyond the round wash tubs with hand-cranked wringers, sat the disassembled Model-A Ford. While never confirmed, I believe this vehicle became my grandfather's chariot of choice during his dalliance with bootlegging toward the end of prohibition. Details and stories are scarce, but once of age, he taught me the applicable driving skills, especially the "bootlegger's turn."

The eastern wall enclosed three massive bins for grain storage accessible from the outside. In front of the bins were countless stacks of wooden crates filled with iron and steel earmarked for recycling. How they never toppled on me while climbing, I do not know. In the front corner, to the right of the large sliding door, lay the remains of a giant cedar tree harvested to construct my grandmother's closet. Above this tree trunk, in the corner, a ladder crafted of rungs nailed directly to the wall, extended into the heavens of the hayloft.

Each ascent, brought a pause to enjoy the acidic aroma released by crawling over the cedar's trunk. My grandfather was a grain farmer, not a rancher. He left behind the days of keeping livestock, so most times the loft sat empty. At other times he leased it for storing the neighbor's hay bales. Empty or full, the expansive floor and vaulted ceiling provided ample fuel for a child's imagination.

Directly to the west, adjacent to the barn, stood a massive empty, stave silo. The poured concrete had long since bleached and the rusted steel bands colored my hands orange with every touch. As a small child standing on the ground looking up, it appeared to not only reach the clouds, but extend through them, into the land of giants and geese with golden eggs. If the silo ever had a roof, it had long since vanished. Labeled too dangerous, my grandparents warned me not to play in the barn or silo, for fear of a fall, cut, or getting trapped between or under the stacked items. This warning extended to not disturbing the family of snowy owls, two adults and two babies, who made the barn their home during periods of migration.

I feel certain my grandparents, especially my grandfather, knew better. Despite the warnings and cautionary tales, they could not keep me from my explorations. The old barn transformed into my castle and the silo, my stone tower with its chute, my turret. From there I would embark upon the most magnificent quests a small boy could conjure. Despite a fear of heights and the perilous uncertainty of the rusted hardware and wooden rungs, I would climb through the chute to the top of the silo, and sitting upon the turret, survey my kingdom. Stretching far as one could see, the lush, green, enchanted lands extended to the north, and to the east, the open plains lead to where the monsters roamed. The golden hills rose sharply in the south, and in the west, a raging river sharply cut through a dark and mysterious forest. Within these realms, my exploration cultivated a creativity, playfulness, and imagination I now take for granted and exercise far too little.

Despite flat fertile soil, my grandfather would never plow under the northern enchanted lands. Each spring, as the new grasses sprouted, a series of compacted rings magically formed across the field, highlighted by the fresh growth. A village of teepees once adorned the field and called these lands home. Our family would walk amongst the circles and explain the largest ring in the middle belonged to the Chief's teepee. Following storms, my explorations of the northern enchanted lands would encounter clay pipes, arrowheads, and other artifacts uncovered by the rains. The items were never collected and left to remain with the soil and the spirits who enchanted the world I now roamed as a curious visitor. Sitting within the various rings, I would envision their daily lives and discussions, as the children snuck around the long gone, circular hides on adventures of their own.

Only rarely did I embark upon adventures in the eastern realm. The lack of trees increased the peril of exposure along the arduous journey, a long two mile trip to the rock quarry. I would hide among the mounds and crevices, watching as giant metal monsters lumbered through the valley, carving out rocks and throwing them into piles. Some days I envisioned dinosaurs driven by cavemen. On other visits, I watched as horrific beasts fought with weapons of boulders. I did not take this realm lightly, for when the monsters gathered in the south, it would not take long before they awoke the slumbering giant. More than once I became sidetracked. I invoked every ounce of energy to complete the terrifying sprint back to the castle before a piercing scream filled the air followed by an eerie silence. Within moments, the earth trembles and emits a thunderous, explosive noise, as the giant erupts like an enormous mushroom and angrily pelts the valley with dirt and debris as if mimicking a hail storm.

The golden hills of the south were as benign as the eastern realm dangerous. With little of interest, the south did not fuel the imagination. Endless waves of grain would give way in late summer to unsteady clods of plowed dirt, with no trees and nothing to explore. An occasional barbed wire fence complicated the journey. The sloping field moved steadily upward to another farmstead. The only challenge was to sneak across the golden hill, enter the realm and touch the opposing kingdom's castle, below their brilliant quilted crest, then scramble back to my kingdom without detection. My grandmother, puttering about the kitchen, enjoyed a complete view of the golden hill and the neighbor's barn through the window above her sink, making adventures in the southern realm less challenging and more self-defeating.

By far, I spent the majority of my adventures in the western realm. A cool, clear creek winding through a massive tree line separated an expansive field, lush with the pungent, sweet mossy smell of alfalfa. This was my raging river and ancient forest. I crafted a base camp beneath an old bridge, stocking it with a blanket, canned food with a can opener, fire kit, and extra clothing. With the camp as my staging area, I explored every inch of the creek and tree line. I transformed the old homesteads and outbuildings into mysterious ruins of far off lands. Frogs, toads, and all manner of critters represented enchanted beings inhabiting a magical province filled with uncertain terrain and danger around every bend. More often than not, even with back-up clothes, I returned covered in mud to face a cold, forceful garden hose before gaining permission to enter the house.

As a lone adventurer traveling within uncertain territory in far off realms, knowing your specific location and remaining time before sunset is critical for safety. The weakest of light can illuminate obstacles to navigation and identify the scope of travel, prior to night descending. Around farms, grouped and single coyotes are frequent predators. Within my imagination, they were always a pack of wolves on the hunt. The safety of the house was essential once the sun set and darkness crawled across the land. After all, growing up we learned what wolves do to little pigs and children visiting grandmothers.

Not all explorations occurred within far flung realms. I had plenty of adventures closer to the castle. An old nearby grain bin, no longer used, served as my rocket ship and enabled me to travel the stars and transform the farm into alien terrain for completely brand new adventures. The original house where my mother was born had long been torn down, but the root cellar remained. The rows of shelves and wooden bins, unused jars and hooks in the ceiling, easily transformed into labyrinths, catacombs, and mad scientist laboratories for battling monsters, vampires, and mummies, or seeking out hidden pirate treasure. During rainstorms, I would often remain in the barn, imagining the snowy owls as majestic griffins guarding my castle. Or pretend to be caught in quicksand while trudging atop the stored grain. Within the grain bins, I learned to trap vicious animals and alien creatures using potato chip cans sunk into the wheat. Once in position, I rarely had to wait before netting the prize of a new friend or pet for a few hours, then let the mouse loose for another day.

Despite the adventures surrounded by far off realms and transformed scenery, my grandfather's workshop earned the most magical place to explore. An aging two-car garage, peeling with faded sage-green paint, set nestled between the house and the barn. Across one wall were built-in wooden bins. Within each cubbyhole was nestled greasy gears and bearings of extraordinary shapes protected by thick, waxed Kraft paper. Another wall supported multiple shelves with jars, hanging by their nailed lids. Throughout the shop sat workbenches, power tools, and various mechanical wonders under repair. The air felt thick with industrial smells from multiple flammable substances, all competing for dominance. The aged, warped wood projected a dark luster possible only from decades of abrasive polishing by greasy hands. Each receptacle and each corner revealed fascinating tools and materials to nourish a young boy's fertile mind, giving birth to a multitude of wonderful ideas.

My grandfather enabled my imagination and creativity through hours of crafting components and accessories for play. I still have the medieval knight broadsword and ninja short sword he helped me build. My grandmother, just as empowering, taught me to sew and cobble bits and pieces into wonderful costumes to legitimize my adventures. Never is imagination as alive as when it is properly accessorized.

Sadly, the Kingdom of Troy no longer exists. My grandparents have long since passed and the farm has changed owners many times. Never able to afford it myself, I still venture back to the old county and drive by a few times each year to survey what remains of my imaginative childhood. The silo, my tower with a turret, stands as tall as it ever did. Unfortunately, the barn, my majestic castle, has now fallen into ruins. Lost shingles and damage from livestock have exposed the old growth wood to the relentless and unforgiving Kansas weather. Long torn down, my grandfather's garage appears to me as a ghost within the empty space it once stood. The old root cellar is filled in with trees planted over the top. In the east, the monsters have vanished. The rock quarry closed once its exploitation of the land was complete. The raging river in the west flows much smaller than I remember, and nearly non-existent from continuing drought.

Though saddened by the present state of affairs, all is not lost. Many of my grandfather's tools now adorn my own workshop, including the well-worn bench grinder and anvil used to construct my swords. I still call them to duty in service of creativity and imagination. My children have the same passion for sewing and creating costumes, toys, and items for everyday use. Soon they will pass those skills to their own children. Unfortunately, living in cities, we do not have the privilege of castles or towers. Exploring outer realms are fraught with new perils, unsafe for fertile minds and innocent play. We now rely upon parks and family vacations to fuel inspiration, build magic, and give life to imagination.

A Kansas native, Troy Robinson recently retired from State service. After nearly 40 years of technical instruction and writing involving lesson plans, training manuals, policies, and investigative reports, he is now exploring the world of creative writing. His poems Legacy Lost and Glory were published in The Tulgey Wood, Vol. 52, 2023. He is a member of the Kansas Author's Club, District 6. This is Troy's first published short-story.

What's Your
Take On Snakes?
Chuck Warner

Back in the 1970s our close friends left Lawrence for a new job in Wichita. The couple and their two young boys moved into a rental house in Whitewater, a nearby small rural community located northeast of Wichita in Butler County. Tall trees shrouded a stately old house on a sizeable lot that backed up to the Whitewater River. Soon after they moved there, they were invited to attend a neighborhood potluck and cookout. During the picnic, the subject of mice came up. Everyone complained about battling those abundant little rodents in their homes. Our friends looked at each other and proudly announced. "We don't have mice!" and were promptly informed, "Then you have snakes!"

Their new neighbors explained how the banks of a small stream are excellent homes to a variety of critters looking for food and shelter in nearby structures and all old houses in Whitewater have plenty of small structural openings to accommodate numerous uninvited guests. For most of their neighbors, it was mice and their absence suggested that snakes had moved in.

After the party, our friends went home in disbelief, wondering, how could they have snakes and not have seen them? Still, out of an abundance of caution, that night they quietly crept down their basement stairs to see if they might have possibly overlooked an unwanted reptile. After carefully searching the entire basement without finding any unwelcome pests, they finally lifted their eyes to the open beam ceiling.

Lo and behold, they were shocked to see several snakes slowly slithering between the open joists. (Okay, I might have overdone the alliteration.) Horrified, they looked at each other in disbelief. Reminiscent of the snake pit scene from the first Indiana Jones movie, the thought of their two young boys playing unattended in that basement totally appalled them. Filled with self-doubt and loathing, they thought, what kind of parents are we?

My ever-resourceful friend figured he could clean up the problem on his own. So, after he got home from work, he put on his pith helmet, picked up his trusty nine-iron, and marched down to the basement to dismantle the snake colony. Once the victims were clubbed, he dumped them in their poly cart with a sign on the lid warning, "dead snakes."

On trash day, his wife went to the mailbox just as the trash truck pulled up. When the trash hauler opened the poly cart, he stepped back with a startled expression and announced, "Ma'am, those snakes are not dead!" Apparently, my friend had only stunned the nearly two dozen snakes writhing around in the bottom of the trash can.

I assume that after the snakes were hauled off to the landfill, the mice rejoiced and returned to their old house, but our friends moved to Wichita soon after, leaving nature's age-old struggle between mice and snakes to the next occupant.

Who Doesn't Love Snakes?

Okay, the fear of snakes is fairly common. Throughout history, our literature, culture, and religions have traditionally maligned snakes, casting them in an unfavorable light (think the garden of Eden). Also, children learn to fear snakes by watching the reactions of their parents, who learn it from their parents, etc. However, it might be more than poor public relations and learned behavior. One psychology researcher from the University of Vienna studied the pupil dilation of the eyes of human infants when they watched pictures of snakes. She concluded that because the fear of snakes is observable at such an early age, that it might be inherited rather than learned.

Regardless of the source of the fear of snakes, members of the same family are not always aligned. From the beginning, our family—me, my wife Karen, and our daughter Stacey—all resided on the fear end of the spectrum. The only true snake lover in our family was our son Mike, who must have inherited his love of nature from his great grandfather, a naturalist at the University of Kansas Natural History Museum.

Mike's appreciation of animals began in grade school when he began collecting a wide variety of unusual pets. His first was a hermit crab, then he graduated to reptiles: a skink, a line snake, an iguana, and several ringneck snakes. With the ongoing presence of these "non-traditional" pets, Karen's fear began to dissipate, while Stacey and I remained standoffish, at best. Also, in 1986 Karen began teaching second grade in the Lawrence public schools where a section on reptiles and amphibians was part of the district wide curriculum. As a true believer in hands-on education, she intentionally introduced live snakes to her students. So, every year Karen had several cages in her classroom filled with a variety of critters: a bull snake, a glass lizard, a bearded dragon, and a three-foot long prairie king snake.

At the beginning of each school year, Karen encouraged her students to touch and hold the snakes and lizards so the children would learn not to fear them. During that first week of classes, most of the children refused her offer. However, after the fearful ones saw that no harm came to the kids handling the snakes, the rest overcame their fears and eventually could proudly handle the snakes when they passed them around in the class circle. Later in the school year Karen would also offer her students the opportunity to watch feeding time. She only remembers maybe two students each year who declined watching the large prairie king snake skillfully corner the live mouse before swallowing it whole.

Of course, her snakes were all non-poisonous, which avoided the school administration's concern for possible legal liability. Just in case you're wondering, when Karen taught her students to not be afraid of snakes, she also taught them how to identify and avoid the poisonous varieties.

When the summer break came around each year, Karen transported her reptile menagerie from the empty school building to live with our family. Unlike a dog or cat, snakes and lizards never require a lot of attention, except when they escape from their cages. The woman who cleaned our house was extremely cautious when working during those summer months. After learning we had snakes and lizards which sometimes escaped from their cages, any time she walked from one room to another, she carefully peered around looking for runaway reptiles.

Like our house cleaner, our daughter Stacey wanted nothing to do with those "icky and slimy things," a common misconception, as Karen reminded me. On the other hand, Mike liked reptiles so much that when he was in junior high school he joined the local herpetological society, where the other members were older boys and men. At one of their meetings, they asked everyone to bring something for "show and tell." Mike loves to tell the story about when was his turn, he slyly smiled and slowly pulled up his pant legs to show off his snakeskin cowboy boots. Who would think that a true "herp" devotee would have such a dark sense of humor?

Stacey was especially squeamish about snakes at dinner time. Let me be clear, not our family dinner time, but the time of the week when the snakes were fed. One time Karen and I were out of town and Mike was unavailable, so we asked Stacey to feed the critters. Karen had a live mouse on the menu for the prairie king snake. Visualizing the three-foot snake wildly thrashing around, chasing a baby mouse in an enclosed glass aquarium before being devoured alive was simply too much for Stacey's vivid imagination. As a result, she couldn't bring herself to do it. However, concerned that the snake might starve, our teenage daughter got the bright idea to drive over to the local pet store and trade the live mouse for a "pinkie" (seriously, that is the official name for frozen baby mice sold in pet stores). With the snake calmly swallowing its frozen prey like a large inanimate capsule, Stacey had successfully avoided the trauma of viewing nature's version of "hunger games."

Karen remembers only two times snakes escaped from their cages at school. Several days after the first snake had gone missing, Karen was instructing her class when they heard children screaming across the hall. She smiled and told her class, "I guess they found our snake." The snake had apparently slithered across the hall under the cover of nightfall to another classroom where the children and teacher were not as comfortable with snakes. Karen immediately went to retrieve her snake and she found a chaotic scene; all of the students were standing on their chairs shrieking and the teacher had positioned himself as far away from the snake as possible.

The second incident occurred another year when a snake was gone so long, Karen presumed that it, like Elvis, had "left the building." However, a few weeks after the escape, as Karen prepared her classroom before the children arrived, she heard the principal using his most official voice over the building intercom, "Karen, please come to the office. I found your snake." When she arrived at the office, the principal pointed with contempt and trepidation to the bottom drawer of his desk. As she opened the drawer and gathered up the snake, she smiled and reminded the principal, "At least we don't have a rodent problem."

CHUCK WARNER has lived in Lawrence since first attending the University of Kansas in the 1960s. With business and law degrees, he embarked on a nearly forty-year career inbusiness and banking before retiring in 2008. After a 2009 family reunion and a behind the scenes tour of the KU Natural History Museum, he began exploring the idea ofwriting about his maternal grandfather and in 2019 *Birds,Bones, and Beetles: The Improbable Career and Remarkable Legacy of University of Kansas Naturalist Charles D. Bunker* was published by the University Press of Kansas. In 2020 his book was recognized as a Kansas Notable Book, won both the Martin Kansas History Book Award and the Looks Like a Million Book Award for best book layout from the Kansas Authors Club, and was a finalist in the High Plain Book Awards.

CATHY MARTIN, OIL ON CANVAS

Barry and the Deer:
David Hann

My friend, Barry Billings told me this story, saying "This could be the story of my life." I think he was talking about doing things without thinking them through.

had this idea that I was going to rope a deer, put it in a stall, feed it up on corn for a couple of weeks, then kill it and eat it. The first step in this adventure was getting a deer. I figured that, since they congregate at my cattle feeder and do not seem to have much fear of me when we are there (a bold one will sometimes come right up and sniff at the bags of feed while I am in the back of the truck not 4 feet away), it should not be difficult to rope one, get up to it and toss a bag over its head (to calm it down) then hog tie it and transport it home.

I filled the cattle feeder then hid down at the end with my rope. The cattle, having seen the roping thing before, stayed well back. They were not having any of it. After about 20 minutes, three deer showed up.

I picked out a likely looking one, stepped out from the end of the feeder, and threw my rope. The deer just stood there and stared at me. I wrapped the rope around my waist and twisted the end so I would have a good hold. The deer still just stood and stared at me, but you could tell it was mildly concerned about the whole rope situation. I took a step towards it...it took a step away. I put a little tension on the rope and then I received an education.

The first thing that I learned is that, while a deer may just stand there looking at you funny while you rope it, they are spurred to action when you start pulling on that rope. That deer EXPLODED.

The second thing I learned is that pound for pound, a deer is a LOT stronger than a cow or a colt. A cow or a colt in that weight range I could fight down with a rope and with some dignity. A deer? no chance. That thing ran and bucked and twisted and pulled. There was no controlling it and certainly no getting close to it. As it jerked me off my feet and started dragging me across the ground, it occurred to me that having a deer on a rope was not nearly as good an idea as I had originally imagined. The only upside is that they do not have as much stamina as many other animals. A brief 10 minutes later, it was tired and not nearly as quick to jerk me off my feet and drag me when I managed to get up. It took me a few minutes to realize this, since I was mostly blinded by the blood flowing out of the big gash in my head.

At that point, I had lost my taste for corn-fed venison. I just wanted to get that devil creature off the end of that rope. I figured if I just let it go with the rope hanging around its neck, it would likely die slowly and painfully somewhere. At the time, there was no love at all between me and that deer. At that moment, I hated the thing, and I would venture a guess that the feeling was mutual. Despite the gash in my head and the several large knots where I had cleverly arrested the deer's momentum by bracing my head against various large rocks as it dragged me across the ground, I could still think clearly enough to recognize that there was a small chance that I shared some tiny amount of responsibility for the situation we were in, so I didn't want the deer to have it suffer a slow death, so I managed to get it lined back up in between my truck and the feeder - a little trap I had set beforehand ... kind of like a squeeze chute. I got it to back in there and I started moving up so I could get my rope back.

Did you know that deer bite? They do! I never in a million years would have thought that a deer would bite somebody, so I was very surprised when I reached up there to grab that rope and the deer grabbed hold of my wrist. Now, when a deer bites you, it is not like being bit by a horse where they just bite you and then let go. A deer bites you and shakes its head almost like a pit bull. They bite HARD and it hurts.

The proper thing to do when a deer bites you is probably to freeze and draw back slowly. I tried screaming and shaking instead. My method was ineffective. It seems like the deer was biting and shaking for several minutes, but it was likely only several seconds. I, being smarter than a deer (though you may be questioning that claim by now) tricked it. While I kept it busy tearing the bejesus out of my right arm, I reached up with my left hand and pulled that rope loose.

That was when I got my final lesson in deer behavior for the day. Deer will strike at you with their front feet. They rear right up on their back feet and strike right about head and shoulder level, and their hooves are surprisingly sharp. I learned a long time ago that, when an animal like a horse strikes at you with their hooves and you can't get away easily, the best thing to do is try to make a loud noise and make an aggressive move towards the animal. This will usually cause them to back down a bit so you can escape. This was not a horse. This was a deer, so obviously, such trickery would not work. In the course of a millisecond, I devised a different strategy. I screamed like a woman and tried to turn and run.

The reason I had always been told NOT to try to turn and run from a horse that paws at you is that there is a good chance that it will hit you in the back of the head. Deer may not be so different from horses after all, besides being twice as strong and three times as evil, because the second I turned to run, it hit me right in the back of the head and knocked me down.

Now, when a deer paws at you and knocks you down, it does not immediately leave. I suspect it does not recognize that the danger has passed. What they do instead is paw your back and jump up and down on you while you are lying there crying like a little girl and covering your head. I finally managed to crawl under the truck and the deer went away.

So now I know why when people go deer hunting they bring a rifle with a scope so that they can be somewhat equal to the Prey.

DAVID HANN HAS WRITTEN MANY STORIES, articles and books. *Bluebirds to Tikal*, 2023, *The Jayhawker Cleveland*, 2021, *River Memoir* and other stories, 2011, and *Kansas Past: Pieces of the 34th Star*, 1999.

Hann established himself as an aficionado of the strange wonders of Kansas in *Sampling Kansas: A Guide to the Curious, 1990.* David lives in Lawrence, Kansas, where he retired from the University of Kansas in 2009.

BLUEBIRDS TO TIKAL | DAVID HANN
ISBN-13: 978-1-960462-01-5
Publication Date: 8/30/2023 | 5.5 X 8.5; 222
pages; $21.99

Recommended For Art, Nature, And Science Fans!

This is a book for art lovers, designers, and art-loving techies everywhere! A coffee-table art book filled with lush art plates that speak to the senses, the fractal images within reflect the beauty and mystery of the natural world, and demonstrate the power of computer-aided design in creating original works of art.

Acclaim for Fractals:

A NEW CATEGORY IN DIGITAL ART EMERGES. Cleveland's work can be classified as a new form of abstract art since they represent objective realities through layers of elements that achieve striking effects. You can say that fractal art is unique, but it begs the bigger question of what makes it unique compared to other art forms. As a fractal artist, Cleveland demonstrates how it can be unique, for it is the only medium that explores fractal structures through digital and classical aesthetics. Browse through this collection and experience its mesmerizing effect.
—*Vincent Dublado, Readers' Favorite*

ISBN-13: 978-1-941237-29-8 $46.49

"I was blown away by the pieces of art the author has created. This is one of those art books that one needs to keep close to the favorite coffee place and relook at the art work every now and then. If you love fractals, you will love this book."
—*Mukesh Gupta, NetGalley Reviewer*

LIMITED COLLECTOR'S EDITION BOOKS & SELECT ART PRINTS ARE AVAILABLE THROUGH THE ANAMCARA PRESS WEBSITE IN SIZES SUITABLE FOR FRAMING.

(C)JMaino

JOSEPH MAINO, PHOTOGRAPHER

PART II—
POETRY

SILKEN THREADS

Poems submitted for the SUMMER 2023 edition of *The Write Bridge* include revealing the secrets of men and women, weighing clouds, perilous attractions, stepping bravely into the ring, deciding whether or not to pull the trigger, finding pathways, moon pies, what we can and can't control, and more.

AMANDA MCCOLLUM

Hunting Alone:
Kelly W. Johnston

Alone in my deer blind, I
watch and wait while daylight
holds, and a bit after. Strong
coffee and crackers help keep me
alert, as hilltop shadows march
across the prairie. I can be as still
as a cottonwood – bare arms
holding up the sky. Deer know
the first to move is the first to die.

I used to hunt with a companion.
He began hunting in the jungles
of Vietnam. He survived but brought
home wounds. He refused to pick
up a firearm for years. In dreams
he was still killing. When I began
deer hunting, one day he decided to join.

The call of the wild beckoned him
to the Chautauqua Hills, as it did me.
Sandstone bluffs, oak forests and big
bluestem provide sanctuary for wild
critters, and our unquiet thoughts.

As sundown reddens, my attention
no longer tracks to his blind. His scars
have claimed him. His ashes feed
the prairie. My watch finds crows calling
reveille, and bluejays stealing corn
from deer feeders. I imagine a thick
tall pair of antlers emerging from
a grove of slender fingers of sumac.
I may or may not pull the trigger.

Kelly W. Johnston is a life-long Kansan. He graduated from WSU in 1977 with a creative writing major in the English Dept. He studied under Tony Bobin, Anita Skeen, and L.M. Grow. He attended law school at Kansas University, and took a long haitus from creative writing. Kelly began seriously writing again in 2007. Since then, he has published poems in The I-70 Review, The Flint Hills Review, and The California Quarterly. He has published two chapbooks by Blue Cedar Press: *Kalaska* in 2017 and *Tumbleweed* in 2020.

Haiku:
Annette Hope Billings

Still in his velvet
a buck stands in the clearing
inhaling wood smells

RONDA MILLER PHOTO

We would like to introduce you

to a Meadowlark book...

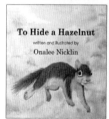

MEADOWLARKBOOKSTORE.COM

105 MEADOWLARK READER
A Kansas Journal of Creative Nonfiction

Meadowlark Press LLC
Publishing Award-Winning Titles by Midwest Authors since 2014

The Season Of Believers:
Mark Scheel

"It is wrong always, everywhere, and
for everyone, to believe anything upon
insufficient evidence."
~ W.K. Clifford

Let me tell you a secret:
men and women alike,
at certain times, for recurring reasons,
(more than even securing salvation)
crave to be seduced.
Not, mind you,
by the purveyors of lust,
but rather by the dispensers
of faith. We are,
after all, the beneficiaries
of the gods and heroes
of Joseph Campbell. Whether from pulpit
or crystal ball, love letters
or hustings, how we do
relish good myth.
And if you question
how this can be so,
consider the following parable:

> *There was once, one mere lifetime ago*
> *a youth who went forth in*
> *the night streets of Fillmore*
> *in quest of magic dust*
> *for his sweetheart. The streets*
> *were dark and strange and lonely,*
> *and finally this youth met up*
> *with a Johnny boy.* The Johnny boy's*
> *suit looked oh so pretty; his gold*

tooth gleamed when he smiled.
The Johnny boy inquired as to
the object of the youth's search
and immediately volunteered
his expertise.

He said he understood the need.
He said he had a sweetheart himself.
He said he had connections.
He said he'd be willing to help.
He said he could tell how they'd
         both had a hard life.
He said they were alike.
He said both of them deserved much better.
He said in truth he loved him like a brother.
He said if you can't trust your brother,
         who you gonna trust?
He said he'd take care of all the arrangements.
He said all he needed was the money.
He said, brother, all you gotta do is wait.

Thinking of his sweetheart
waiting in their love bed, the youth
entrusted his last ten dollars
to the Johnny boy.
Doffing his hat gaily, the Johnny boy
departed . . . never to be
seen again. And the youth waited.
And waited. Alone amid
the dark streets. Until
empty pockets and rage
devoured his effervescent faith.

But rage, unlike faith,
is a transient emotion.
Hence, the lessons of youth
are left behind with youth.
And so the first Tuesday in November
finds us all butt-deep in placards
bartering our hopes and dreams
with the Johnny boys.

O season of believers!
You beautiful dreamers!

W.K. Clifford must be
spinning in his grave.

Mark Scheel, from *Star Chaser,* 2020, published by Anamcara Press. Mark grew up in east-Kansas farm country. Prior to writing full time he served with the American Red Cross, taught at Emporia State University, was an information specialist with the Johnson County Library.

Me? Hose-Less:
Ronda Miller

him? camouflaged
we stand
cliff's edge
end of our world
boxed in
shoulder to shoulder
head to head
toe to toe

never seeing
eye to eye
eating
our half
a moon pie
hard to swallow
chocolate
decadent
take the dive
a jagged fall
freedom?

blink of an eye
hand in hand
land
each other's space
passion ignites
sharing
lover's embrace
tension gone
grievances forgotten
individual egos forsaken
delight in the 'us'

Ronda Miller

The Hide-Behind:
George Gurley

A woman wakes up in the middle of the night,
thinking she's heard a strange sound.
She gets out of bed, walks down the stairs...
(Troubled music)
"Hello? Hello?" she says. "Is anybody there?"
As if the intruder would answer:
"Yes, I'm here, hiding. I've come to kill you."

We who are watching cry out:
"Don't go, don't go, you're in danger. Call 911."
But she won't listen.
She keeps walking to her doom.
We realize it's just a convention.
But it never fails to hook us.
The woman reaches the first floor
and picks up a baseball bat.
It will be of no use when she's attacked from behind
by the assailant in the hooded sweatshirt
wielding a machete, an axe,
a syringe loaded with a knock-out drug,
or a cloth saturated with chloroform.

Maybe the sound she heard was just a tree
scratching against a window.
But the patio door is open.
On the kitchen table, a half-eaten orange.
This time, it may only be a concerned neighbor
who'd picked up a key hidden beneath a flowerpot.
More likely it's the jealous mistress,
the jilted boyfriend, the psycho granny,
the neglected stepsister,

or the cheerleader who got cheated

out of being prom queen.

But the real intruder is the Hide-Behind,
a fabulous creature that follows wherever you go.
You can never see it,
because no matter how fast you turn around,
the Hide-Behind is faster and is always behind.
So you go through life seeing only
what appears in front of your eyes.
But should you turn around
and catch the Hide-Behind,
what would you see?
Nothing. The void.

The woman keeps following her flashlight.
Next, we see her begging for her life.
"You don't have to do this," she cries.
"I can help you...If it's money you want..."
Later in a remote spot,
the murderer gives her a shovel
to dig her own grave and says,
"When God closes a door,
He opens a window."

Of course, rescue will arrive at the last moment.
The evildoer will end up
handcuffed in a paddy wagon.
But that's not what happens in real life.
In real life, you finally meet the Hide-Behind
face to face.
Another name for the Hide-Behind is Death.
Another name for Death is Nothing, No-Thing.
At last you see what really is or isn't there.

Note: Lumberjacks, alone in the woods, lived in fear of something that was always behind them, and were known to drink heavily, because alcohol was said to repel the "Hide-Behind." In a poem by Eugenio Montale, the speaker "turns around" and experiences a terrible vision: Behind him is "Nulla, il vuoto." Nothing, the void. Then the "usual deceptions" return: houses, hills, trees. With his secret knowledge, the speaker re-enters to the world "among men who don't not look back." In his discussion of the poem, Italo Calvino introduces the "Hide-Behind," to elucidate the vision of Montale.

GEORGE GURLEY WROTE A COLUMN for the *Kansas City Star* and was Book Review Editor for a number of years. Two books of poetry: *Fugues in the Plumbing* (BkMk Press) and *Home Movies* (Raindust Press)...One book of columns (with Peter Simpson) *Press Box* and *City Room* (BkMk Press). Two plays: *Cures* and *Indian Givers*, both produced by Park College and directed by Pulitzer Prize winner Charles Gordone. Gurley lives on a farm in Kansas where he and his wife Susan have been working on a native prairie restoration project for 20 years.

THE GRIEFMAKER | GEORGE H GURLEY
ISBN-13: 978-1-941237-88-5
Publication Date: 6/26/22 | 5.5 X 8.5; 268 pages; $21.99

Subscribe to *The Write Bridge Biannual Literary Journal*

https://anamcara-press.com/
subscribe-to-the-journal/

H e had tried to get out of Kansas. He had tried to hate the state. He'd joked about the 'Ski Kansas' poster that depicts a desolate, flat landscape, featureless except for a broken windmill and a scrap of tumbleweed. Kansas had nothing. No mountains, no sea, no metropolis. Busloads of senior citizens didn't come to Kansas to witness the turning of the leaves. There weren't any trees. The wind could blow for days with a punishing will that drove settlers to madness and suicide. Drought, dust storms, blizzards. The Great American Desert. Empty spaces without dimensions or shadows. Visitors from other states experience panic when they enter Kansas—agoraphobia. The first sighting of the blue mountains shimmering in the Colorado distance excites cheers and spasms of relief..."
—*George H. Gurley, The Griefmaker*

"Much in the style of the sweeping works of Cormac McCarthy or Ian McEwan, we take a philosophical look at American values and the struggle of what it is to be American via Gurley's epic story. ...Gurley delivers an intricate, character-based portrayal of two very specific men and their conflicts, struggles, fall from grace, and attempts to claw their lives back together, but on the wider plane, there's an important message about the heavy price of progress brewing in the modern world. What results is an exceedingly well-penned, dramatic slow-burner of a tale that will have you truly gripped and deep in thought by its conclusion. ... highly recommend." — *Reviewed By K.C. Finn for Readers' Favorite*

"George Gurley has the eye and ear of a poet. His descriptions of the weather, the landscape, the wild animals set the stage for the adversities and aspirations of the prairie state." — *Playwright Frank Higgins, "The Sweet By 'n' By, "Black Pearl Sings."*

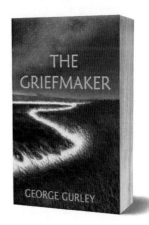

"The novel's inciting conflicts— between personal histories, rare and teeming ecologies, and commercial progress—are fascinating." —*Karen Rigby, Foreword Reviews*

"This is a spendid story set in the American Midwest" —*David Garrard Lowe, author "Lost Chicago"*

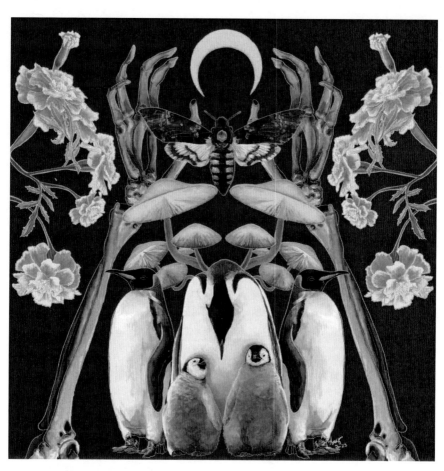

AMANDA MCCOLLUM

A Fat Woman Considers Clouds:
Brenda White

The average cloud weighs 1.1 million pounds,
and I thought I was fat.
Why I'm merely a droplet
held next to a cloud's mass,
a feather's fractal if you will.

Yet I can drive through clouds
resting on the ground,
and no one can drive through me
—— without incident.

I jiggle and bobble as I navigate earth
while clouds wisp across firmament
like ghosts in slow motion
metamorphosing shapes and statures
until they touch Heaven
or vanish altogether.

I'm pinned to the earth by gravity,
by my body's rolls of excess.
Why can't I be free as a cloud,
drifting like an angel through atmospheres?
Simultaneously porous and opaque.

I guess I'm not willing to be a million pounds
heavier.

BRENDA L. WHITE is a graduate of ESU. Her work has appeared in Quivera, The Flint Hills Review, The Write Bridge, and Meadowlark 105 Reader. She writes poetry out of necessity.

When Did You First Realize You Wanted To Be A Helium Balloon?

Julie Ann Baker Brin

Oh, you know, my teenage
years, definitely. I was so
deflated; there was all this
angst, heaviness, low morale.
But I knew somehow, in my
heart, my lungs, that I was
more flexible. That I could
embrace lightness, breathe deeply,
rise above. I could expand
my horizons and maybe inspire
others to do the same. I envisioned
a world of multicolored beauty,
everyone floating, laughing, gasping
in surprise, embracing the sky.

By day, Julie Ann Baker Brin works in broadcasting: not behind a mic, but behind red tape. By night, she prefers to use the other brain hemisphere. She's an award-winning Kansas Authors Club member. JulieBrin.org showcases her works from '105 Meadowlark Reader,' Flying Ketchup's 'Night Forest,' WSU's 'Mikrokosmos' and more.

Millie:
Tyler Sheldon

Sammie's dog, bigger than Sam
is tall, is afraid like death of pool
noodles. When we knock, she
lets us in, and Millie, this mastiff
one could saddle like a horse,
sees us come in and waits,
locked in place by a single
foam tube wedged in the open
door. She whines as though
this simple toy has threatened
her family, or taken her treats,
and later she eats with one eye
on the bowl, and one on the door,
feeling the noodle's spectral
presence. We watch her from
the couch. When later we leave,
Millie looks out from under the
foam, a finger curved above her
like the ghost of Christmas Yet
to Come, and we tell her no,
we cannot take you with us, and
we tell her, be brave, and
pet her head, and she somehow
steels herself, and gazes back at us
with the courage of a thousand dogs.

Tyler Robert Sheldon is the author of six poetry collections including *When to Ask for Rain* (Spartan Press, 2021), a Birdy Poetry Prize Finalist. He is Editor-in-Chief of MockingHeart Review, and his work has appeared in *Dialogue: The Interdisciplinary Journal of Pop Culture* and *Pedagogy*, The *Los Angeles Review, Pleiades, Tinderbox Poetry Journal,* and other places. A Pushcart Prize nominee and winner of the Charles E. Walton Essay Award, Sheldon earned his MFA at McNeese State University. He lives in Baton Rouge, where he teaches, writes, and usually has a cat on his lap. View his work at TylerRobertSheldon.com.

Bed Making:
Lindsey Bartlett

-For Ivy

The black and white Pitbull accompanies
me while I make the futon bed. I grab sheets
from a drawer, shaking them from folded
shapes. Thinking it all a game, the Pitbull
darts from corner to corner as I tuck ends
under soft mattress. White paws bat at my
hands as I spread the blanket. I could be irritated
with her antics, making play from my work,
banish her, and close the door. Make the
bed in peace, but to me that would diminish
what humans can learn from these animals
we domesticated. That life is more than a
series of tasks, a list of boxes to check.
Instead, learn from a black and white Pitbull
not to take things too seriously, even bed making.

Bartlett teaches composition and literature at Emporia State University. Bartlett's poetry can be found in her book, Vacant Childhood. Additional writings and photography have appeared in The Milk House: A Rural Writing Collective, The Write Bridge, Flint Hills Review, and 105 Meadowlark Reader.

AMANDA MCCOLLUM

Amanda "Haiku" Nunes:
Beth Gulley

The fighter
doesn't dance around.
She goes straight
for the takedown.
The fight is done
48 seconds
into round one.
Viewers are left
thinking "I paid
for this?" and
"I need to see
this fight
a few hundred
more times."
Announcers are
left speechless
and unprepared.
It's like reading Basho
for the first time.

Beth Gulley was an Amity literary prize finalist in 2023. The contest is sponsored by Anamcara Press. Beth Gulley lives in Spring Hill, Kansas and teaches writing at Johnson County Community College. She has published two chapbooks and three full-length collections of poetry: *Since Corona Ruined Our Trip to the Library* (Finishing Line Press), *Little Fish: Tiny Meditations on Freedom* (Flying Ketchup Press), *Dragon Eggs* (Spartan Press), *The Sticky Note Alphabet* (Alien Buddha Press), and *Love of Ornamental Fish* (Alien Buddha). Beth serves on the Riverfront Reading Committee and is a Writer's Place board member where she edits the yearbook. More information about Beth can be found on her blog at https://timeeasesallthings.wordpress.com/.

Southwest Idiom:
Gretchen Cassel Eick

He hid
behind a cloud
like a war torn,
butterfly
down in New Mexico.
His u-joints failing.
Boy, the old kid
leaked more than a bad
transmission.
Later the sun
painted that Yankee face pinto.
He said,
"the Buffalograss
called to him."
I sooner believe
His cornbread
ain't done in the middle.

Visiting and living in other countries shapes Gretchen's life. She taught in Latvia and Bosnia and Herzegovina and worked for 14 years as a foreign policy lobbyist. She wrote two award-winning scholarly histories and five novels (the latest, Dark Crossings, 2022). She was Kansas Authors Club's Prose Writer of 2021.

Decision Tree:
Patricia Cleveland

Looking down from the crown
You can clearly see
The path from the bottom
To the top of the tree
Looking up and on
it's not so easily done
All pathways are open
Til you finally pick one.

Twice Told Tales
104 South Main Street
McPherson, KS 67460
(620) 718-5023

Everything We Can Control:
Diana Silver

Owls screech us awake. Coyotes
yip-howl through all the dark months.
They pause at our windows at night.

In this human compound, apartments
stack on hills surrounded by forest
on the brink of the Plains.

Last winter a mountain lion stood
beside my porch, her paws
darkening snow. We locked eyes.
Breath slid in and out until she turned
and walked into the woods.

If she wanted to wait hungry at my door,
I couldn't stop her. If coyotes took
my cat, I couldn't save him.

I saw a doe in the yard this morning
strolling with the indolent laziness
of a shopper at a farmer's market.

She crossed all three blocks of buildings
quickened her pace, trotted to where
the highway waits.

I ran onto my porch, waved my arms,
shouted. She didn't stop. She didn't
even hesitate.

Silver is a Pushcart Prize-nominated poet and performer who seeks to tease open the scar tissue life layers over our hearts. She has been published in Ms, The Progressive, MockingHeart Review, The Lavender Review, The Coop, and many other places. She can be found online at dianesilver.substack.com.

Perilous Attraction:
Anna Bartkoski

What is this attraction?
What keeps drawing me in?
Why do I feel the need
to indulge in this perilous sin?
You'd think I'd know better,
old enough to change how I act,
acknowledge my reality,
distill the fiction from the facts.
You'd think I'd care more about
the consequences I've faced,
about the state of my soul,
which has all but been erased.
You'd think I'd learn to listen,
for my own sake, to obey when
the world tells me no,
when my children beg me to stay.
You'd think a lot of things,
some true, others not so much.
You'd think I could bear life's
weight without this disastrous crutch.
You'd think I'd toughen up,
quit acting the bitch, fix myself,
mend what is broken, sew myself up,
stitch by stitch. You'd think I'd choose
differently. Desire foremost to finally live,
become enchanted, loving and playful,
realize how much I have to give.
You'd think I'd step up, allow myself
another chance, but the needle always

draws me back with her promise of sweet romance.
You'd think I'd think of time, how little I have left.
You'd think I might choose life
over this depleting, poisonous death.

Anna Widener Bartkoski: Anna has been writing for 20 years, stopped writing for awhile, then her muse found her again. She loves running, reading, knitting, and everything related to food and cooking. Anna loves to be outside and prefers to live life barefoot.

And I Pray:
Chris "Diaz"

As a young teen
I ended up taking a pledge.
I fell in love with the streets and
livin life on the edge.
The OG's would lace me
with nothin but knowledge.
This type of schooling
you could never find in college.
Riding in a tahoe, smoking
a blunt full of indo. On the other
side of town with a gun out the window.
"Shoot him!" were the words the homie
had said. So I let one go as I
aimed at his head. I don't know
what the results were that day.
I still talk to God about this
as I pray.

Perilous Grace:
LeAhana Hunt

Frying chicken strips turned
perlious in an instant as flames
danced on top of the grease.
My friend's face displayed
my fear as our talking and laughter
Suddenly cease. Wondering what
to do, we did nothing, the flames grew
with a playful grace. Reality jolted
me out of my hypnotic state. 'I have
to make the flames go away!'
Water did not work and time would't stop.
I picked up the pot, air ignited
the flames, fear threw the pot in the sink.
Somewhere internally, I admired
the beauty of the flames.
The fire now out, but my skin…melting.

Stop Crying! Nicholas MaGee
I'm teasing in a perilous way.
What is this meaning, I can't quite say.
I use drugs, conceal guns, fear and money.
Sweet to me as bread and honey.
Hit your lights.
I don't stop, fuck the cops.
I flip you off. Bending corners
is how I dip, posted on your block
is how I sit.
What's my problem?
A key unlocks answers.
What solution dissolves?

I sleep and I wake,
the sun rises and falls.
Bones and earth
restructured.

rain cloud pouring
gravity collapsing
nebula
I am rich with boils and sores.
I am rich with no hair.
I am rich in my thin frame.
I am rich with this weakness.
rich with the thought of only one
way to beat this.
Nothing but nothing.
Death is my cure!

LeAhana Hunt began writing in 2022. She plans to write a book entitled I Believe prompted by her battle with addiction and her belief that sometimes the difference between making it or not making it is whether you have someone who believes in you when you cannot believe in yourself.

Weapons Hanging Outside the School Cafeteria:
LaDeana Mullinix

Like baby teeth in a baby dragon
they grew, inverted trees forging a new
linear ring with each re-freeze.
These ice fangs stretched
to twice the size of the child
whose hand I held.

Fierce, menacing, they could impale this boy,
drawn to them, of course,
by their glittering glory and danger.
We knocked a few free --
too heavy to hold and slippery,

and returned each day
in the lengthened winter sun
to see them self-destruct,
melting to a pool
of sparkly dragon drool
by the side door.

Killer in Plain Sight:
Jalia Bruce

Masterminds that can only be criminally defined.
Masked assailants that attack with all graphic,
painting pictures in full acrylic,
applying layers of paint, colors that darken
the crimson shade of hate.
Crimes of passion create patterns of deceit,
bludgeon the soul. Murder on the mind
blindsides current thoughts.Telling familiar lies,
dying screams pierce the air
leaving soft whispers of rationality.
The body count begins to rise
every thought to go back retracts
from its original path.
Lurking in the shadows
biding their time, they become victims
of their own mind. Look deep in their eyes.
You'll find the soulless killer living in plain sight.

Confession:
Brian Daldorph

I've given details of the three bodies I buried in my garden.
"But you live in an apartment," the detective says.
I'm moving on to killings at Rest Stops on the highway, a lot of foolish people
park away from the lighted zones.
"How many victims, Daniel?"
"Fifteen, at least. Five more last Saturday. In Kentucky."
"Have you got a driving license, Daniel? Have you ever had a driving license?"
"One more in California. This week."
"Have you ever been to California, Daniel?"
"I drove there on Tuesday."
"You've never driven a car, have you, Daniel?"
"I took the bus."
I wonder how the press will play my story: If it bleeds, it leads,
and I've caused a lot of bleeding.
"I did a lot of killing in the war too. Atrocities."
"The Civil War? The First World War?"
"Both," I say. "I just couldn't stop."

BRIAN DALDORPH teaches at the University of Kansas and Douglas County Jail. He edits *Coal City Review*. His most recent books of poetry are *Ice Age/Edad de Hielo* (Irrupciones P, 2017), *Blue Notes* (Dionysia P, 2019), and *Kansas Poems* (Meadowlark P, 2021).

Artist's Angst:
Heather Duras

I woke up irritated.
I feel in need of reinvention.
(Or is it intervention?)
My paintings mock me with their mediocrity.
So I'm writing about them in revenge.
Maybe I will paint over all of them and start again.
Like a Biblical Flood of Gesso.
The Colonial(ist) Spirit
I'd like to own a landscape
A real Vista, a MEGA View.
Maybe a mountain or two.
I have a Lawn. Two manicured rectangles
(I'm told are bad for the environment)
I plant them round with native plants
for bees and butterflies
Not ants.
I hope to find some concession
for my transgression. But still.
I'd like to own a landscape.
Dust to Dust
how silly of me to lay a claim
to any piece or parcel of this planet.
o call it Mine is
False Divine.
I will one day die and go back to it,
my dust joining your dust.
Do we add any square footage?

A Vision:
Joseph McGovern

Into the shades of night I can only catch a glimpse of light
Truth, I work at this fight
Only to hold my heart from taking off in reckless flight
Searching for reality
Appearances: age beyond this figure since youth

What color do your eyes hold?
It's not beauty, held within a poker game, players can't fold
A circumference when observing justice appears bold,
Visions, standing between self essence
With a repugnant apparition, cleaved together like benign tumors, become my quintessence

A single question remains relaying like a track runner circling my mind…
Your eyes imprisoned in light, what colors are you hiding behind?
Could the intertwining create an eternal binding bridge?
Will pupils be a shade of blue, clear as sky, or darker than my suede shoe?
But not murky, like the vast lake I dove in a wet dream, the first time you appeared

No, brown, like the bark of pine,
Supply wood I chop to warm thy heart containing a winter chill
Green? Like soft thicket moss we cushion heads upon, with a day perceived
Curious – hazel, colors transform among travels,
While depths of your soul – slowly…unravel

But elegance you behold is covered up o'er the lovely pair bestowed
Unmask your wondrous shades, so I can see what colors of your heart are followed

Joseph McGovern was an Amity literary prize finalist in 2023. The contest is sponsored by Anamcara Press. J.A. McGovern is a published poet, songwriter, and independent filmmaker. A graduate, with a bachelor's degree in forensic science - chemistry focus with criminal justice minor, J.A. McGovern currently works as an analytical inorganic chemist. Founder and curator of the literary art anthology "Perception" his artistic team has received multiple nominations and awards for their work. In 2018, J.A. McGovern received an American Songwriting Award for lyrics in folk music, for his independent film's title song, "All Over Again." "Words Left Unspoken" is J.A. McGovern's first poetry collection publication.

Watermark Bookstore

Since 1977, Watermark Books & Café has been Wichita's Home for Books. As a local business, we value our customers whether online or in the store. Beyond selling books and welcoming you in the café to meet (or make) a friend over coffee or lunch, we connect to the community through donations, in-kind, volunteer, or financial. We sponsor author events featuring bestselling and soon-to-be-bestselling authors. We collaborate with non-profits, other local businesses, schools, churches, libraries, and other organizations that make our community what it is. Since 1996, we have been an anchor for the Lincoln Heights Village Shopping Center at the southwest corner of Douglas and Oliver.

Battleship:
Samantha Moon

Standing at the stern in dappled light, a shield
slung across his back, heavy with iron, wood
and muddy flaking paint made from mulberries,
water and beetle shells, sweat beads along his brow,
the nape of his neck, the sun-bleached hairs curl
and tangle into knots. Amber waves roll
beneath a darkening cornflower sky littered
by black-bottomed clouds laden with rain. A low
rumble echoes across the golden bay and
his hand drops to the roughly wrapped hilt of a sword,
useless but steadying as the storm creeps overhead.
Lightning cleaves the air, sharp and hot. Each quick
forked tongue a brilliant pop of white and silver,
shot with blue and the smell of copper. A streak of light,
yellow and dim, flickers steadily near the horizon
between the sheets of cold rain now sliding under his
collar, soaking the drawstring tie of his patchwork cloak.
Gusting winds deliver a familiar and beckoning voice and
he sighs, the end of his journey pulsing ahead in time
with his own ragged heartbeat.
One, two, three... the light blinks and stays, then
One, two, three... again.
He shrugs off his battle-worn gear and jumps off the
starboard side, feet-first into the rain-plastered
grass of the abandoned lot. "Momma's flashing
the porchlight," he shouts as he runs, the neighborhood
crew groaning as their friend is called home.
The great pile of fallen trees and forgotten bricks, some
days a ship and others a castle or a cave or a coliseum,
unfurls its sails as he disappears behind the front door.
"Onward, sailors!" shouts its new captain.

Sam Moon is a Kansas writer and reader. When she's not busy working toward her Masters degree, she can be found burrowed in a blanket with her Kindle and two adopted Boston Terriers. She's a KU graduate and enjoys a career in local government.

BARBARA WATERMAN PETERS

The World Has Lost Its Color:
Thaddeus Dugan

Days flash in the mirror
The same day there
Now disappears
Somehow into the now.
An imposing dark mass
Accumulates in the west
Droplets thud next to my footsteps
Leave dimples in the dirt.
Breeze breaks into wind
And the sopping violence
Slaps against my skin
Until the silence, drips
On occasion.
The rain gauge brims
From the passing storm
And so it warns of the peril
From further downpours
If I continue to neglect the excess.

So I dump the contents,
But now,
There is only emptiness,
And I can't stand that even more.

Thaddeus Dugan was an Amity Literary Prize finalist in 2023. The contest is sponsored by Anamcara Press. Dugan's poem is featured in his debut collection and can be purchased in February through publisher Anam Cara Press. You can find him on Facebook as TA Dugan. Watch for an upcoming authors page and website.

Shadows Remain:
Edward Lee

Sometimes we didn't
have time to shower
before we had to return
to our spouses, our hours
limited by the depths of the lies
told to buy that time.

Those times, our skins
unclean and yet purer
than they'd ever been,
I felt less guilty, the
smell of you on my body
easing my conscience
when my wife asked me
how my day had been
and I lied as easily as though
my tongue had been born
to tell anything but truth.

What cruel people
we were in our love
for each other. What
cruel people we had to be
to save our love
for each other.

We wish our others well
now that we are gone
from their lives, our cruel selves
no more, now that
no false words are needed
to disguise our truth, though

their shadows remain
as such shadows always do,
like dirt on the skin
that an ocean of showers
can never remove.

EDWARD LEE'S poetry, short stories, non-fiction and photography have been published in magazines in Ireland, England and America, including *The Stinging Fly, Skylight 47, Acumen, The Blue Nib* and *Poetry Wales.* His play 'Wall' was part of Druid Theatre's Druid Debuts 2020. His debut poetry collection "Playing Poohsticks On Ha'Penny Bridge" was published in 2010. He is currently working towards a second collection.

He also makes musical noise under the names Ayahuasca Collective, Orson Carroll, Lego Figures Fighting, and Pale Blond Boy.

His blog/website can be found at https://edwardmlee.wordpress.com

Presented to

CHAD BOUGHMAN

Harbor Springs, Michigan

The Fall of Bellwether

• • •

2023 WINNER

The Amity Literary Prize, by Anamcara Press

AC
PRESS

Five Hares in July:
Craig Sweets

This Evening in my walk I saw five hares!
Thimd, fecund, fertile, plump, pert,
Introvert, their ears alert.
And poetic creatures—Chaucer's Monk's "vair"
Which lined his robes—Cowper owned a hare too.
His "Epitaph," with gentle laugh, declares
That his rabbit's foot makes a fine "lucky shoe,"
But never fit for rabbit stew!

*In the Middle Ages, "vair" was fur, used to line a coat.

When he's not writing, Craig works at the Audio-Reader Sensory Garden (on cmpus) is the founding editor of Change of Heart, a streetpaper for and by homeless people in Lawrence and Douglas County for over twenty years. Other interests include classical music, visiting alpaca farms, and local history (e.g.: the Underground Railroad).

Van Gogh:
Ronda Miller

Van Gogh from aloft
creates a masterpiece
impasto magico

RONDA MILLER, PHOTO

AMANDA MCCOLLUM

What's Up With My Bae?
Patrick Sumner

My Bae is so fine
You couldn't touch her man,
There's no way.
She's outa site,
she's tight
she's plain cold to be,
Like Mr. Clean with a magic eraser fool,
she's gonna tear off a piece a clean your sink.
She's not afraid she's No player hater,
She's ferocious if she wants to be.
She's on fire she's sick she's ill she'll make you
wanna go take an extra pill.

Yeah see that's right she has extra sight
she's so bright, That she needs shades
on her Third Eye that glimpses all day and all night.
She's awake she'll surprise you
like your favorite treat, the one's you hoarded
when you got home from Trick n' Treaten.

No worries if she's tired, she'll take a lengthy nap,
I don't care what she does it's a blessing to my soul,
It never gets old. She's bold do you know what I mean?
She's wearing a bumblebee jacket can you even hack it?
In the presence of greatness what you gonna do?
You need to go over rover,
step to your management office your rent is due.

Yes she's cold, play
she's partially made out of ancient clay.
She's hot got it? She's got It.
She should be on the cover of Vogue
you damn rogues
Always with your wondering
About this and that.

She ain't got no time for you.
She has goals, she has plans
I'm chill I'm in her hands.
Move along there's nothing to see here.
I know it's hard not to glance,
as when she walks
it looks like a dance.

Patrick W. Sumner is a social and political activist in Metropolitan Kansas City.

While a youth in Kansas City, Missouri, Sumner was involved in the punk rock music scene. He attended Penn Valley Community College, as well as the University of Kansas where he earned a degree in American Studies with an emphasis on Great Plains culture in 1997. He and his brother, Brandon, produced several award winning documentaries including an exploration of alleyways in *Rear Entry*, and *Civil War on Wheels*, which explores the world of demolition derby. Sumner taught social studies and African American history at Central High School in the early 2000s. Sumner has been an advocate and leader in a wide variety of reform issues in areas such as education, prisons and community building. He was a member of the Kansas City chapter of the NAACP and a representative for the Volker Neighborhood Association, among other various organizations and movements.

Subscribe to *The Write Bridge Biannual Literary Journal*

https://anamcara-press.com/
subscribe-to-the-journal/

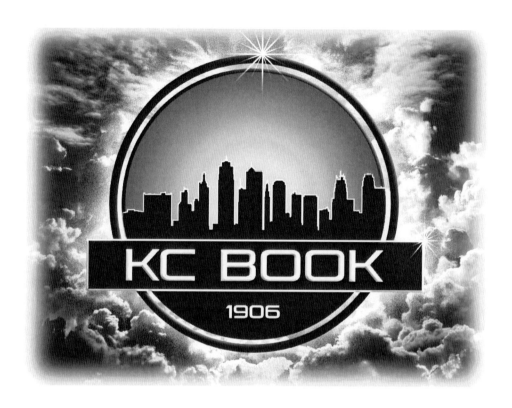

COMMITMENT TO OUR CUSTOMERS

Established in Kansas City in 1906, the KCB management team has a combined total of 125 years work experience. This kind of commitment is passed along to all of our customers on a daily basis as we produce your orders.

KCB believes every step is important. Service, quality and price are all equally important at KCB. We pride ourselves in working as a team to give our customers the best product for the lowest price in the shortest amount of time. Throughout our history we have demonstrated our continued commitment to team up with our customers and suppliers, delivering the best books on time.

HISTORY

In 1906 Park Printing was founded by Frank E. Park, and was located in the 200 block of 8th Street in downtown Kansas City, Missouri. During the Great Depression, Park Printing—like the rest of the country—experienced economic upheaval with the crash of the stock market. With the onset of WWII, Park Printing experienced leaves of absence from some employees for military service. Despite the hardships, Park remained in business.

In 1949, Park Printing was sold to John Smith with six employees and one Webendorfer press. By 1960, Park Printing held major clients such as Hallmark Cards, AT&T, and SWB.

The Company is still family owned and operated by Rick Smith. The company changed its name to KC Book Manufacturing to show the centralized location and work performed.

PRINTING

Although KCB has long been a leading source for books, technical manuals and educational materials, our facilities and expertise can provide a wide spectrum of printing services.

Contact us today

KC Book Manufacturing
110 West 12th Avenue
North Kansas City, MO 64116
816-842-9770   kcbookmfg.com

kcbookcustomerservice@kcbookmfg.com

BARBARA WATERMAN PETERS

PART III—
TALL TALES,
SHORT STORIES
& ONE ACT PLAYS

YARNS

Fiction submitted for the SUMMER 2023 edition of *The Write Bridge* include a chilling tale about ice, a story about a bounty hunter with a magical bodyguard in "Sloane Takes a Holiday,"; a tale featuring Morris "who doesn't remember his nude forays," a view of a lake bottom in "Come October," a letter from hell written by Anders Celsius as imagined by Leonard Krishtalka, a cautionary tale about revision in "Servants of the State, and a play in one act about a duck race by former Kansas Poet Laureate Kevin Rabas.

The Fall of Bellwether

THE FALL OF BELLWETHER IS THE WINNER OF THE 2023 AMITY LITERARY PRIZE AWARDED BY ANAMCARA PRESS. I WAS ALSO A FINALIST IN THE SCREENCRAFT'S CINEMATIC NOVEL COMPETITION, 2023

Chad V. Broughman

In the small town of Bellwether, where prejudice and judgment prevail, five harrowing life paths collide and a saga of survival, defiance, and unyielding human spirit unfolds.

"*This story has some really fascinating portrayals of time and place, especially as readers follow along with this anxiousness and tension early on that only continues to spiral and grow, allowing... an extreme sense of build-up that is due in part to the pacing, which is structured so well. I found myself developing intensely personal connections to characters...*" —ScreenCraft Competition Judge

With masterful strokes, Chad V. Broughman transports readers to northern Michigan ... immersing them in a world of duplicity and struggle... With vividly depicted settings, complicated characters, and haunting themes, this historical fiction masterpiece weaves a mesmerizing tale of love, forgiveness, and the power of solidarity.

Broughman breathes life into the fictional town of Bellwether, spinning a web of superficiality and unbending religious beliefs, trapping each resident in its thin, gossamer strands. Authentic dialogue serves as a siren's call, drawing readers into this exquisitely sculpted tale that exalts love, forgiveness, and communal bonds... this literary gem stands as a testament to the indomitable resilience of the human spirit, a reverberating reminder that through unity and boundless compassion, the most foreboding shadows can be vanquished.

Ice:
Chad V. Broughman

If I tiptoed, terror would win, and I'd turn back. So I sucked in through my nose then pushed out through pursed lips, still trekking forward. Thin gray puffs of breath whirled and burned off in the bitter wind as I marched across the uneven expanse of ice. Every time I thought about the frozen lake beneath my feet, I turned my mind to other things, like the latest wasteland of fake news, the unpaid insurance bill, or my son's full eyes and little, warm hands. My new sled scraped dutifully behind me, jostling against the rigid folds, bouncing its contents: a 12-gallon bucket with camouflage seat cushion, a "state-of-the-art" tip-up still wrapped in plastic, a corn-flower blue auger snagged on Facebook Market Place, and all the tackle some cocky, twenty-something salesman from the sporting goods store insisted on. I felt good about mysupplies and pretty roughneck in my new Carhart overalls and jacket. I'd always thought that was the mark of a real badass, a man who buys his clothes from the local tractor-and-seed supply. Still, every step forward was a battle, a test of true fatherhood. My legs shook, not violently, but enough to heckle me, never letting me forget that I was scared shitless. This isn't about you, I chided myself. Cowboy up.

It was just after sundown on a February night in upper Michigan. Pink-purple swaths smeared the sky, blending with the meager starlight just enough to illuminate the paths where other fishermen had tramped. At least twenty yards from shore, well past the point of no return, sat two shanties, both seemingly empty, like desolate cabins on a prairie, abandoned during hard times. Folks seeking better places, better chances. There was a lone Northern Goshawk circling overhead, giving rapid-fire warning of a possible threat, a round of "ki ki ki ki ki's" wobbled across the otherwise silent stretch.

Cautionary lines from all the how-to videos turned in my head—"clear ice is strongest" and "never go by yourself." The former was a best-case scenario, a crossing of fingers for optimal conditions. And the latter, well, that wasn't going to happen. I had to fumble through the ins-and-outs of this ice-fishing racket alone, field my way through the risks, the pitfalls. Only then could I teach my son with a head held high. Or at least be able to fake some courage with a slice of believability. Samuel, my seven-year-old, had unknowingly pistol-whipped me with his words, yet again: "Justin's dad takes him fishing on the ice. Why don't we do that?" He'd have caused less damage with a swift punch to the balls. All my self-doubts and inadequacies rose like bile. Those round irises, though. So brown, so rich. I remember asking the doctor when Samuel was born if peepers were supposed to be that big. I made sure to split the difference between the shanties, situating mine at least a stone's throw away. Not because I was practicing any YouTube ice-fishermen etiquette, but rather fearful they might not be empty after all, that someone would watch through the flap, witness my butterfingers as I took a first stab at this. As I unloaded the duffle-bag, a frozen thunder-clap boomed across the open space, like the ice had split in two. I paused, listening to the lake groaning as if it was sick. The instinct to slip the straps back over my shoulders and scurry back to shore loomed large. But I resisted, inhaled the brisk air and let it burn my lungs. Then I dumped the tent from its bag and pulled on the sides until they clicked into place. I took off my gloves to light the propane heater, but fifteen degrees is brutal in a treeless plane. Soon enough, my fingers were stuffed back into their moisture wicking mitts.

Another rumble from below. This one raced the length of the lake, zipping by like a freight train. My heart felt as if it might pound its way into my mouth. And my stomach began to clench. I took in another wintry gasp, held it, then let it go while reaching for the auger. It took some doing but eventually the dull blades punched through. I heaved upward, and a rush of water and ice chunks spread out from the hole. It was a good feeling. I had set up a jig before-hand, so I pierced a couple of waxworms through the hook, watched them squirm, then wiped their biscuit-colored guts on my bibs and dropped in the line. I reeled it out with a twelve-count, just the way the thick man with the red mustache and throaty voice did on the Michigan Outdoors Channel. "So you think you want to ice fish?" he'd asked, staring down the camera as he'd loosed his reel with one hand and stroked his grassy whiskers with the other.

The hawk squawked another round of ki ki ki's into the gloaming, now faded to royalblack. Even so, I could see my breaths dissipating into the even-tide like little phantoms. I donned my headlamp, then stopped so I could hear the wind howl through. Thin blue light shone on the milky ice— the stillness was spiritual. I understood why men say such endeavors are their church. The image of bringing home a hard-fought catch pulsed through me like firewater. I pictured my son's prideful grin as I held up a slew of slick, golden-yellow perch, dorsal fins fanned out like mini umbrellas. And I remembered the time I taught myself to drywall because "Justin's dad did their entire house by himself." Samuel's eyes wider than ever, the color of coffee and walnuts. Desperate to mud the smoothest joints of all time—well, more seamless than Justin's damn dad's at least—I slathered on the compound as if frosting cakes for a wedding reception, each coat needing more sanding than the last, swipes of plaster swelling high, starting to resemble the Porcupine foothills. Afterwards, upon first seeing Samuel's new room, my wife gasped, then chuckled, made a joke about goiters. But she drew silent and cast down her head when I didn't laugh.

My pole bobbed, jolted in my grip. It was ethereal. I set the hook, counted to three and yanked up my first catch. A rock bass. Flat body, as if it had been ironed. Face was blunt, nose stubby. Gray-green and spotted all over. In the low light of my lamp's LED bulb, its eyes were red, glossy. I set it against the ruler engraved on the edge of my sled—eight inches. A keeper, barely. Ridiculous to be smiling like a child, I thought. Even more absurd that a snicker slipped out. I unhooked it with my pliers, cursed at it for swallowing the hook so deep. I lay it down, watched it toss and flop. A bit sadistic, but all part of the game. For a moment, I wondered if it could feel fear, self-doubt. Or if it could only live in the moment. No looking back, no looking ahead.

Next, a small-mouth, according to my species chart. And I called to mind the gruffy old man at Young's Party Store as he put the cottage-cheese container full of bait in my palm,

"These fidgety buggers'll catch anything with a fuckin' fin," he'd rasped. Then he crushed out his cigarette, ducked behind the counter and began rummaging, a ream of expletives pouring forth, a unique blend of "fucks," "cocksuckers" and "shit-asses"—the man's life story revealed in the span of a dozen syllables. When he reappeared, there were two Phillips screwdrivers in his hand, both a bit stripped. He must have read the puzzlement on my face. "You're a fuckin' greenhorn, ain't ya? Trust me, put 'em in your damn pocket. If the time ever comes, you'll know why I give 'em to ya." I nodded, shoved them in my overalls.

Six keeper fish in all. A beautiful mix of perch and bass, plus a single ornery pike that bit me when I bare-handed the hook from its mouth, a red line forming in the crotch of my thumb and index finger. I was far from empty-creeled, certain to warrant some laurels at home. Then, the loudest ice kaboom yet. It traveled the path I'd taken out, all the way to shore. And my trepidations reignited like gas to flame. The idea that mere inches of ice was the only thing

keeping me from plunging feet first into the murky, frigid water bulleted to the forefront again, making my bladder pang. With that, I gathered everything onto my sled and shouldered the shanty straps. Deep down, I knew it was only brain tricks, that the last blast hadn't ruptured the trail to my truck. Still, I took a wider route back, veering toward a jut of land east of the launch, trying to avoid the rifts, now a mile wide in my imagination.

I skated toward shore. One foot, then the other, before I dropped like a boulder. Never envisioned it that way, like sitting in a dunking booth and someone's ball strikes the target. It was always slower in my mind, a gradual sinking. The reality was the current tugged at my lower half like a magnet and my hands scrambled to latch onto something, anything. I'd walked across a weakened patch of ice, fed by warmer spring water. Falling into it like all the research had cautioned against. Chest under water, I pawed at the ice, keeping my head just above the surface.

With each grope, my hands slid backward. I was a frantic dog, unable to find its bone. Though I wasn't gaining traction, I wasn't losing any either. But with each passing second, my waterlogged legs grew heavier. So I stopped moving, praying the idleness could steady me, if only for a moment. I lifted one arm at a time, slipping free of the shanty's nylon straps. Though the chill had begun to whelm, I could still feel the heft as the laden gear let loose, drifting down.

With all the stirring, I slid further, too. Water fingered my neck and chin. I tilted my head back to keep my mouth free. And I kicked and kicked. Then my foot caught. Weeds, I thought. After jiggling more, though, I knew that I had tangled myself in the metal ribs of the shanty that I'd just released.

Stars poked through the darkness like tiny flashlights against a threadbare blanket, their shine offering a morsel of consolation as I held stock-still. As sure as the numbness set in, I knew I couldn't tread much longer. There was a fleeting flash of warmth as the piss swirled around my groin. Only then did the cold truly register—my cheeks, my nose, my ears. I tried calling on God to calm my thrashing heart, that's when the string line full of fish floated beside me. Samuel would never see my catch. The beautiful, dead pike lingered near, starlight reflecting from its creamy white underbelly. And I couldn't stop the tears.

I wondered if God was answering me after all, giving me permission to die. A half dozen cars had gone by, and I tried picturing the drivers' faces, maybe listening to the Saturday country countdown and singing with their spouses. Or someone texting a lover, trying to stay inside the lane. And me, hovering like driftwood mere yards away. My eyes closed, and I saw Samuel's face, his penny-hued gaze, that devil-may-care smirk.

An inexplicable surge shot through me like a fire-bolt. All at once, I was someone else, someplace else. Without thinking, I plunged below, scrambled to untangle my foot. It was darker than I'd imagined, still something loosened. But when I twisted upward, I lost direction.

Couldn't have gone far. The opening had to be just overhead. I pushed on the ice from underneath in a lake-weighted slowness, my eyes bulging. The terror crashed and plucked as I fought to hold my breath. Strange how I could sense my own wits flattening. A spasm tore through my spleen, and I summoned God again. He did not come as a winged caricature. Nor in some artist's romantic rendition. Rather, I felt Him, everywhere. In the brilliance of Sirius. In all the sky. He refracted through the ice, into what would surely be my freshwater grave.

I felt myself starting to let go, heart fluttering like pondweed. That's when I felt the tip of one of the screwdrivers jab my thigh. I jerked both from my pockets. And my face struck the ice—a sickening, remarkable thud, unlike any friction I'd ever known. I knew the cut was deep. I was grateful that I couldn't see the blood, the torn skin. I dug the steel shanks into the wall above me, pulled myself hand over hand until I saw the light where I'd first fallen through. With all my might, I cleaved toward the opening until my arm rose out of the water, into the air. Then, I thrust my head back into this life, gasping like a newborn freed from the womb. I stabbed both screwdrivers atop the ice and hoisted my upper half to safety before going slack, breaths dissipating like cigar smoke. I rolled onto my side, spotted my truck. So damn close; a world away.

As I trudged to shore empty-handed, a semi passed by, interior lights on. The driver didn't notice me, never even turned his head. I stripped down to my longjohns. My teeth chattered hard, felt as if the enamel was crumbling like bread crust. The key was still in the visor and with a trembling hand, I tried putting it into the ignition but missed, again and again. Finally, the engine roared to life. I couldn't feel the flesh of my back against the seat, so I cranked up the heater, catching a glance of myself in the rearview mirror. The gash on my forehead crooked to just below my left eye, and the blood had frozen, ropy and rusted against my temple. The icicles that had formed in my hair were melting down my spine, into the crack of my ass. And my inhales were still quick, through my nose, then out through my mouth like popped balloons.

I couldn't feel my foot on the gas either, but the speedometer read fifty, the street sign twenty-five. Not sure I could've slowed if I wanted to. Still felt like I was floating, just outside myself. Gravity was tugging, but there was no bulk for it to lock into. My innards were hollowed out. Scaffolding and bone.

I see-sawed past our drive, slid sideways into a snowbank. Don't recall opening or closing any doors. As I lumbered toward the house, the Chevy still sissed behind me, and the dome light glowed a cloudy yellow in the periphery. Once inside, I plodded past my wife sitting on the couch, wrapped in the afghan she'd crocheted herself, wavy patterns of kale green and bell pepper orange. Vanna White was on the television, flipping those big block letters, smiling wide as a circus jester. I tried barreling up the stairs, forgetting my legs were still wooden.

Rather, I banged my way to Samuel's room, heat from the furnace pricking my nerves alive.Before entering, I paused, drew in a warm breath, then crept inside.

There he lay.

Open 'em, son. Just a glimpse of your beech-bark eyes, that's all I need. I knew they were flitting behind those tiny lids, watching big dreams unfurl. My heart squeezed like a dishrag, and a sob burst free, one I'd been holding since I was born. I bit into a knuckle, only stopping when tooth grated cartilage. I could hear my wife calling for me, her feet pattering up the stairs. "Honey? What's happening?" Her voice cracking with panic. I bowed my head, rubbed my forehead with my palm. And the wound reopened, drops of life pooling on the white carpet—red as beetroot in the moonbeams streaming through the window. I daubed at my face, the acrid smell of fish slime flooding my nostrils.

In the hall, my wife's shouts grew louder. "What's happening? There's blood on the—" her words broke off as her footsteps clacked faster, closer. From behind my fingers, I peeked at Samuel again, still gamboling in cloudland. More beads spilled down, across my eyelid, landing on my lips. A deluge of saltiness seeped onto my tongue, rich and metallic. But this time, I defied the impulse to wipe away the mess— the sacred, beautiful mess.

Previously published in Etched Onyx Magazine, Winter 2023.

Chad V. Broughman is the winner of the Amity Literary Prize, 2023, by Anamcara Press, for *The Fall of Bellwether*. He was the recipient of the Rusty Scythe Prize Book Award and the Adobe Cottage Writers Retreat honor in New Mexico. As well, Chad was awarded two chapbook contracts for his short story collections--"the forsaken" and "slighted"--both published by Etchings Press. His fiction can be found in journals nationwide, such as Carrier Pigeon, East Coast Literary Review, River Poets Journal, Burningword, Pulp Fiction, Sky Island Journal, and From Whispers to Roars, and he is anthologized in Write Michigan Short Story Anthology, On Loss, and Scribes Valley Anthology. He is a Best of the Net and Pushcart Prize nominee, holds an MFA from Spalding University and served as co-editor for the fiction/poetry blog "Cafe Aphra" based out of the United Kingdom. Chad teaches English and Creative Writing at the secondary and post-secondary levels but is most proud of his roles as a husband and devoted father to two rambunctious young sons.

KATHLEEN KASKA

Another hotel; another murder; another Sydney Lockhart mystery.

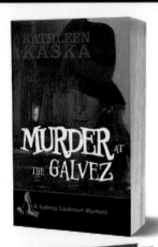

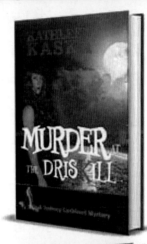

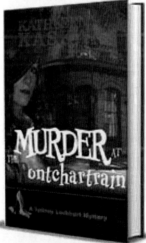

The Sydney Lockhart Mysteries

Sloane Takes A Holiday:
Alisha Diane Ashley-Galloway

A bounty hunter and her magical bodyguard accept a contract to kill a sorcerer

There is a bounty hunter called Sloane. She drives a rust-red, beat-up pickup, and carries a sawed-off shotgun, a bowie knife, and an ancient, yellowing scroll about the size of a cigarette. She only takes a certain type of contract. All magic is illegal, but some magic is more illegal than the rest. Above a certain level, cops and government agencies can't handle it, so they call Sloane. Capture or kill. She generally chooses option two. Her last kill was a warlock who was summoning and imprisoning all the fairies in Vermont, for reasons she never fully grasped. He died before he could finish explaining himself.

They always want to explain themselves. Sloane isn't interested.

Tonight, Sloane's hunting a conjurer who's allegedly been summoning demons. A real no-no. She's driving down a two-lane highway in the dark. Her pickup's headlights flash on the trunks of tall trees and illuminate shallow drainage ditches full of brambles. There's a grand old manor house out here somewhere, or so they say.

It's always a grand old manor house. Sloane shakes her head. Mages, man. Necromancers, wizards, sorcerers. They're all alike. No imagination. Her father was different—

eccentric, manic, broke as shit. They lived in a hovel when she was a girl. There wasn't even a lock on the door to their woodsy shed. It still astonishes her that her father survived long enough for her to kill him. What kind of shitty sorcerer can't figure out a basic health and wealth charm?

Sloane turns off the highway and ambles the truck along a narrow dirt road. A dusty, scratched up street sign reads *Memory Lane*. Cute. The trees here crowd closer. She kills the truck's lights and coasts the last fifty yards, parking in a grove of feathery oaks—a useful landmark if she needs to get out of the manor quickly and run.

She's weary. This late-night shit has got to go. If she could pick a life, it would happen mostly on a white sandy beach somewhere, quiet and peaceful and luxurious. And beachy. But Sloane doesn't know how to make that beach life happen. She's a registered magic user, a known entity. All the agencies have her picture and her profile. They tolerate her so long as she's useful. Her only option is to be the hunter in the story—or else she'll become prey.

Lucky for Sloane, she's a good hunter.

The lock on the front door is easy to pick. The invisible wards around the necromancer's manor are harder to dispel, but she manages. These men think they're protected by wards and acres of young forest surrounding their castles of old stone. They're not protected. Not from Sloane. She checks her weapons and her scroll.

The door creaks open at her push. She drifts into cold silence. The entryway is devoid of any candle or butler to show the way. No matter. Sloane has her methods. She mutters a short incantation. A shadow detaches itself from the corner and wraps around her like a mink stole. Her eyesight sharpens to that of an owl. She loves this spell. Nothing like a shadow cloak and night vision to make her feel badass. She takes stock. It's a standard mansion: high ceilings, and a grand staircase leading up to what Sloane assumes are well-appointed apartments. Rich people always have rooms ready to impress guests, although she doesn't know anyone who'd want to attend a dinner party hosted by a necromancer.

Nobody smart, anyway.

Sloane ignores the stairs and turns down the hallway to her left. The shadow moves with her, keeping her draped in silky darkness. Down and to the left. That's where she'll find him. Sloane worked that out after her first half-dozen kills. Whatever evil muck these assholes meddle with, it affects them all the same. Makes them predictable. If she takes every available left turn and descends every staircase she encounters, she'll find him.

Three left turns and she finds a hallway that feels right, cobwebbed and murky like a tomb. These guys must all hire the same architect. She wishes a necromancer would build his lair in any other kind of place than this. Maybe the penthouse of a skyscraper, or an observatory, or a bathhouse. The gig is getting boring. She runs her fingers across the purple damask wallpaper. Her shadow spell leaves traces like curls of smoke off a candle. Jesus, she thinks. Even their interior design taste is uniform. Did they all subscribe to the same home decorating magazine? The Sorcerer's Study? Lair Wares?

Maybe she should retire, she muses. Go into deep hiding. Let someone else fight the occult forces that threaten to drag the world to Hell. At least then she wouldn't have to look at any more fucking bordello wallpaper.

Sloane is startled out of her reverie by a shrieking ghost. She stumbles back. Her hip strikes the corner of a lamp stand, hard. She swears. Her shadow spell dissipates. The woman—former woman, specter, whatever—hovers six inches off the ground, her face a rictus of horror and grief. For one horrible, crippling moment, Sloane remembers the first time her own face wore the same expression. The day her father was possessed.

But that day, Sloane didn't become a ghost. She became a hunter.

Sloane keeps her cool. Her heart is jumping. She's tempted to cry out, she's tempted to fire the shotgun; it's a motherfucking ghost. But she keeps her cool. The ghost is lit from within, eerie and blue like they all are, and her scream ricochets off the walls and the inside of Sloane's skull. It's not a real sound, Sloane knows. It's a psychic echo. Only she can hear it. The ghost is trying to warn her.

"Yeah, I get it," she says through a tight throat. "Evil lurks nearby. That's why I'm here."

The ghost keeps screaming. Sloane pushes past her, hip throbbing. That'll bruise. Must be getting close.

She finds the stairwell hidden behind a tapestry depicting medieval knights chasing a stag in the woods. If she ever learns where these assholes buy their art, she'll torch the warehouse and sing show tunes until the cinders smolder. She pulls out her scroll and holds it tenderly for a few seconds. Then she unrolls it and gingerly presses it against the wall next to the staircase. It sticks there as if she'd glued it. She murmurs a few words in a dead language and the djinn inside the scroll wakes up. The paper glows orange, like a coal that's not done cooling. Sloane smiles.

"Keep a look out, will you?" she says softly. She touches the scroll with one gentle finger. "Got a monster to kill."

The stairs don't creak. The shotgun is a comfort in her hand. Killing mages is hard work, but Sloane has found that a sawed-off shotgun increases her chances. Her mind sharpens as she descends the long, unlit stairwell. She's an exterminator, she thinks. No different than ridding a basement of rats. Except these rats are bigger, and they're always summoning their rat friends and hosting murder parties. The stairs end in a pool of red, flickering light. Mages and their fireplaces. She's never met one who uses electric lights. Maybe technology interferes with their magic. Anyway, they all have fires. Saves her the trouble of starting one herself.

Sloane creeps into the necromancer's lair. It's a cavernous space, big enough to host a banquet. It's decorated in a gaudy, overdone art deco style, with black and white geometric patterns and gold leaf filigree on every available surface. It's hideous. If she hadn't already planned to kill him, this would have pushed her to it. She half expects a community theater troupe to come out and mangle a few scenes from *The Great Gatsby.*

And there's her quarry, the rat bastard himself, leaning over a table crowded with arcane instruments. The necromancer is reading something, scratching notes in the margins. He wears a hooded black robe, just like in the movies. What a douchebag. Sloane pulls her knife from its sheath. She saunters toward him, ignoring the pain in her hip.

"Knock knock, magic man," she calls. "Company."

He looks up. His face is just a regular face, not the dark visage of an evil mage. He could be an accountant.

"What have we here?" he murmurs. He doesn't seem surprised. They rarely do. Sloane figures men like this are always expecting someone to barge in and demand they stop their twisted magic. It's probably why most of them start conjuring up demons in the first place. For the attention.

Sloane stops ten feet from the necromancer's table, gun hand steady at her side, bowie knife in the other. The necromancer peers at her through his round, wire-framed glasses. Like Harry Potter's. God, she loathes him.

"Whatcha reading?" she asks lightly. Sloane has learned that mages can't resist questions about their books. It's almost a compulsion. Pavlov's necromancer.

"This is the grimoire of Jehoshaphat McCrory," the necromancer says.

"A real page turner, that one."

"You know McCrory?" He blinks rapidly behind his glasses. They could be in a library, talking about bestsellers. But the mage's unflappable demeanor puts her on edge. The maniacs she hunts usually start bloviating about incursions into their blood-soaked, sanctified conjuring spaces.

Why isn't he bloviating?

"You've read one grimoire, you've read 'em all, right?"

"No," the necromancer says. He closes the book. "You are Sloane. Yes?"

"The one and only."

"You have come to kill me." There's something off about his voice. Sloane gets the distinct impression he's about to start some shit. Her trigger finger twitches.

"Sharp as a tack, you are." She levels the shotgun at his

chest.

"I knew that you would come." His speech pattern is strange. It doesn't quite match up with the movement of his lips. It's like watching a samurai movie where the audio has been dubbed over. Except this samurai is an unassuming, bespectacled necromancer with a smudgy quality to his edges, which Sloane suddenly perceives, too late, as evidence of possession.

The demon smiles with the accountant's lips.

Fuck. Sloane's stomach drops.

She tries to pull the trigger but the bastard is faster. He snaps off a spell with a crisp wave of his hand and issues a short, sharp word Sloane doesn't know. A slicer. She drops to dodge it, tweaking her already injured hip. She yelps. Her knife clatters away. The sicko demon riding this idiot got the drop on her.

Anger doesn't cover it. She feels like a grenade with its pin pulled. Sloane is about to go off on this motherfucker. She works up a brutal crushing spell that would make the accountant into mush, but the demon banishes the casting before she can even deploy it.

Okay, she thinks. So he's not gonna go easy. Sloane takes aim from her prone position and pulls the trigger on her gun, both barrels blaring forth directly at the demon's face. The creature inside the conjurer throws up a ward, scattering some of the shot but deflecting most of it directly at Sloane. She rolls away with a millisecond to spare, cheek stinging where a pellet grazed her.

"You are a Magus," the demon says with the accountant's face. "One of the old kind. You've killed many of my friends." He takes off the glasses and smiles again. She wonders why he even bothered wearing them before. Cosplay? Sloane's hip aches, as well as her elbows where she dropped to avoid the slicer, and also, somehow, her soul. It's her father all over again. "I will eliminate you from this plane."

This fucking guy. Sloane's rage spools up into something like a cyclone and she stands, ready to flay the fucker—and the demon flings a handful of sand at her head.

The spell is instantaneous. Her feet leave the ground, her body no longer beholden to Earth's gravity, instead compelled by the monster's will. Sloane is hovering, helpless, and totally freaking out. She tries to reach for her knife, but her limbs won't do as she tells them, and anyway she dropped it before, she forgot.

"I will drain you, little sprite," the demon promises. Sloane is quaking like she hasn't done since the first time she met a demon, the night she killed her father and became what she is. "Your soul will power my enchantments. I will drain you of your magic. I will build a new future."

Here we go. Sloane would roll her eyes if she wasn't panicking in the vice grip of his paralyzing spell. They always want to explain themselves. "Future?" she asks, buying time.

"Yes," the demon says. He steps close to her suspended body. His smile twists the accountant's face into a distorted approximation of happiness that makes Sloane want to vomit. "A future of death and destruction for your people. A future of woe."

"You're a dick," Sloane gasps. The pain in her hip is worse. She feels moisture on her lip. Her nose is bleeding.

The demon spreads his arms wide. His face takes on a beatific look, somewhere between a grin and a prayer. Sloane feels a tug in her gut worse than any pain or dread she's ever felt. He's draining her soul. She can feel it. The cruelty of it is breathtaking. She thought she understood hate before. She sees again the face of that poor shrieking ghost, a woman whose essence he devoured. Sloane's muscles ache with the strain of being held in a living rigor mortis. The ghost had tried to warn her.

"What's your name?" she asks, desperate.

The demon laughs. "That would be telling."

A name. Sloane closes her eyes. She's been so afraid, this demon caught her off guard, but she remembers now—she's not alone.

She whispers a word. A true name.

And her djinn emerges from his scroll and comes blazing down the stairs.

The resulting fracas is loud and bloody. Sloane collapses to the ground in a quivering heap, her muscles slowly unclenching. The relief is so intense, she thinks she might pass out.

She passes out.

She comes to and discovers she is lying in the truck bed, staring into the djinn's sapphire eyes. He's beautiful, bearded, shirtless, and glowing faintly like a campfire. He never speaks.

"Thanks," she says weakly. "Did you burn it?"

The djinn smiles and bows his head. Sloane sits up with difficulty to see the manor is aflame.

"Salt the ashes," she says. The djinn nods. She lays back down and grins. The stars are out. "I've been thinking. We need a vacation. Maybe an island somewhere?"

Her djinn glows brighter and nods. He presses his scroll into her open hand.

Sloane lets her exhaustion drag her to sleep, and she rests the way a child does, with the sweet assurance that she's protected by a monster stronger than anything else out there.

Alisha Diane Ashley-Galloway is a digital marketing strategist and campaign coordinator with fifteen years' experience in social justice and advocacy work. She writes short stories, poetry, and contemplative essays on politics, organizing for societal change, and trauma recovery. She holds a Bachelor's degree in Political Science from the University of Kansas and a Strategic Planning Certificate from UC Berkeley. She lives in Lenexa, KS with her husband Scott and their dog, Everett.

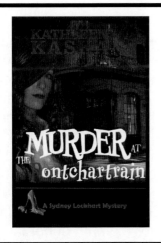

Moris on the Sabbath:
Kathleen Kaska

When Morris was a child, he used to go to church naked, much to his parent's chagrin. Supposedly, young Morris, awakened by the church bells on Sunday mornings, would crawl from his crib while his parents were still asleep and toddle to St. Francis Catholic Church across the street. One of the church ushers would bring Morris home with a subtle reminder to his parents that it might be a good idea if the entire family came to Mass fully clothed.

Morris doesn't remember his nude forays, but hearing the stories told over and over by his family solidified the image in his mind. And because of his early-life experience, now as an adult—Morris could only speculate—he hated wearing clothes on the Lord's Day. Sunday was a day of rest; for Morris, rest meant a day free from all constraints.

So, that's how the embarrassing Easter encounter with Jenny came to pass. Morris was puttering around on his deck, feeling the delicious breeze cool his bare skin, thinking about Jesus rising from the dead. Morris contemplated that miracle as he took down his hummingbird feeder to refill it with the special nectar he'd conjured up from his own raspberries from his organic nursery. Since Morris lived on the end of the island at the end of a dead-end road with his nearest neighbor half a mile away, he was not worried about being seen in the buff. But, on this particular Sunday, just as he snapped the lid back on the feeder, he heard a lovely voice ask, "Excuse me, but is this the Brewer place?"

Morris looked up to see the inquisitive eyes of a stunning young woman staring at him from under the brim of her large straw hat. Before Morris could answer, she posed another question. "Do you add red dye to that liquid? I hope not because red dye is unhealthy for hummingbirds."

Morris quickly hid his nakedness with the pitcher of nectar. "Which question do you want me to answer first?" A stupid thing to say, but Morris wasn't used to having his Sunday routine interrupted. The young lady shrugged.

"This is the Brewer place. I'm Morris Brewer. The sign near the front gate, Brewer's Organic Farm, should have told you that. And I wouldn't think of adding red dye."

"I didn't come from the front gate. Would you like my hat? It would provide a better shield than that clear glass pitcher." When she removed her straw hat and handed it to Morris, the waviest blonde hair he had ever seen fell onto her shoulders. For the first time in his thirty-eight years, Morris felt a little too pudgy, a tad too short, and somewhat too hairy for polite company. Morris reached for the hat but left the pitcher where it was. At this point, two shields seemed like a good idea.

"If you didn't come through the gate, you must have hiked through the woods." He doubted that analysis because his visitor looked like she'd just come from an afternoon tea. Her white sundress, dotted with tiny pink and green flowers, was as fresh and clean as a spring morning. On her feet were delicate pink sandals that seemed new enough to have just come from the box.

"In these shoes? Don't be silly. My name is Jenny Hitchcock. I could use a glass of water or maybe some iced tea. It's rather warm out today. But, of course, you might not have noticed."

Morris did notice, however, that despite her neat, crisp appearance, she looked a little flushed. Something told him the flush had nothing to do with finding a naked man on his deck feeding hummingbirds. Morris began to relax back into his natural comfort, but he had no intention of turning this encounter into a social call. If he wanted to be social, he'd don a suit and attend the Easter Vigil at St. Francis's Church.

Before he could tell this Jenny woman to go on her way, she placed a white-gloved hand on the deck rail and stepped onto the bottom step. Morris couldn't remember ever seeing a woman wearing gloves not meant for warmth.

"Well, I do have some sun tea ready. Sit down over there." Morris pointed to his nice collection of wicker patio furniture he'd picked up a few years ago at Costco. As he backed toward his kitchen, he watched as Jenny Hitchcock studied the cushions of each chair before she selected one that suited her.

Once inside the house, Morris got control of himself. Beautiful woman or not, how dare she barge in here. He was formulating the trespassing lecture he'd deliver when he brought out the tea. He was proud of the words that popped into his head, like gall and traipse and brazen and crass, when Jenny called through the window, "No sugar in mine, please."

"Sugar!" Morris huffed. "Who does this woman think she's dealing with?" Except for his homemade preserves and honey and a gallon of Black Strap molasses, there were no sweets in Morris's kitchen. He plunked ice cubes into two tall glasses so hard that he feared he had cracked one. That's the glass he'd give her in case it had a slow leak. Shame washed over him like Judas before the crucifixion. The metaphor reminded him that he should don an article of clothing himself. He went into his bedroom, and for the first time in ages, he couldn't decide what to wear. How absurd. He had a suit of clothes for every day of the week but nothing for Sundays. Determined not to be put out, Morris grabbed his favorite bath towel, which always made him think of the Shroud of Turin, and wrapped it around his waist.

"It took you long enough," Jenny said. "I thought you said the tea was ready, or did you have to freeze the water for ice cubes?"

Morris walked over and set the tray on the table with a thud. Standing there in a towel, he suddenly felt like a complete idiot. He couldn't remember which glass had the potential crack. He sat down with a sigh, exposing a goodly portion of his left thigh.

"I've heard about your place," Jenny said. "About how you bought it when you returned to the island after college. How it was an overgrown nursery, and you brought it back to life in just a couple years. Impressive." Jenny picked up a glass of tea since Morris seemed incapable of speech.

"Who are you?" he finally found his breath.

"I told you. My name is Jenny Hitchcock. I'm your neighbor."

"Excuse me?"

"I bought the place next door," Jenny said.

"What place?" Morris's ears started to ring.

"The old Perkins place." Jenny emptied her glass and reached for the pitcher. "Is it always this warm in the spring? Not that I'm complaining. I'm from Texas, and it's usually in the triple digits by March."

"The old Perkins place? When did it go up for sale?" Morris felt the muscles around his heart constrict. Old man Perkins had promised Morris he'd never sell. Said he'd donate the land to the Land Bank.

"You're thinking about the Land Bank, aren't you?" Jenny said. "Eli Perkins stroked out last week in the nursing home. Seems he never got around to making the provision in his will. In fact, lucky for me, he never made a will. So the land went up for sale, and I bought it. Drink your tea."

Morris felt himself overheating and wishing for the first time that he had a swimming pool to jump into. He picked up his glass and took a long drink of cold tea when suddenly the bottom fell out, drenching his lap.

As Morris sat there, staring at the ice cubes nestled in his crotch, he had a strong feeling that, for him, life would never be the same.

Kathleen Kaska is the author of the awarding-winning mystery series: the Sydney Lockhart Mystery Series set in the 1950s and the Kate Caraway Animal-Rights Mystery Series. *Murder at the Arlington* and *Murder at the Luther* were selected as bonus books for the Pulpwood Queen Book Group. She also writes mystery trivia. *The Sherlock Holmes Quiz Book* was published by Rowman & Littlefield. Her Holmes short story; "The Adventure at Old Basingstoke;" appears in *Sherlock Holmes of Baking Street*; a Belanger Books anthology. She is the founder of The Dogs in the Nighttime; the Sherlock Holmes Society of Anacortes; Washington; a scion of The Baker Street Irregulars.

Come October:
Ronda Miller

I'm lying face down in the most beautiful lake I've ever seen. Crappies drift by intent on their daily intake of young bass, perch and bluegills, along with mosquitoes and fathead minnows.

It was the crappies that brought us to the lake today. John's promises of catching fish on my first fishing expedition lured me in. A fall day spent in nature, and the fantasy of escaping my house amid Covid 19, almost equaled the thought of spending time with John.

John and I had never seen each other in person before today, even though we'd been communicating through Facebook Messenger for almost a year.

I first contacted John with a phone call about presenting via a Zoom meeting for a group of Boy Scouts. John and I immediately formed a connection.

We had both been raised as small town, country kids and we agreed that most of our pleasurable childhood memories had been experienced within nature. Both of us had lost our mothers early in our lives, John's due to cancer when he was nine, and mine to an automobile crash due to a drunk driver when I was eleven.

I used to scroll through the numerous messages John and I had sent each other, sometimes to refresh my memory on how we'd met, why we'd become friends, and exactly when that had occurred. Maybe it never did occur with John. It might have just been inside my head. I was desperately lonely.

I began learning about John's likes and dislikes. I wanted to please him.

John was a giver. He'd leave venison, ripe tomatoes, sometimes green ones once he learned that's what I preferred, fresh crappie fillets and other items on my porch, then he'd send me a message that he'd done so. I never saw or heard him.

I began reciprocating by leaving items on my porch that I knew he liked, a bag of apples or trail mix, a fresh cantaloupe, homemade cookies, things he could enjoy when he'd leave for days at a time on hunting expeditions.

John would send me photos of himself with his liver and white English Pointer, Bennett.

Sometimes in the photos, he'd be lying down with his dog beside him, sometimes his photos were of a meal he'd cooked or an antic his dog was up to in a nature shot.

John's conversations never became sexual. He frequently spoke about his wife, children and his grandchildren. And I reciprocated with shared information about mine.

I messaged John one day when he was on a hunt to ask him if he'd tell me about killing a deer.

I wanted to learn about that process.

He sent me his phone number a day or so later, before he drove home from a hunt, saying I could call him if I liked, or not, whatever I felt comfortable with.

When I called him, I asked him about the killing process, especially the specifics about what he did if the doe was pregnant. He explained the difference between killing a deer using a bow and arrow or shooting it. He told me how he'd drag his kill into an open space so it could be seen by predators like coyotes, hawks and eagles. He'd leave the entrails and other heavy parts of the deer behind for birds and animals of prey as a way to honor that animal. It completed the cycle of life and gave life to other animals through its death.

He shared the mechanics of how he'd pop a ball joint out of place to make it easier to skin the deer, how he'd slice a roast and wedge it into a snowbank to begin the cooling off process required prior to packing the venison into the cooler he had close at hand.

What he didn't tell me, what I wanted to know, were his emotions as his hands moved across the still, resplendently warm body of the deer as it twitched spasmodically - reflexes still functioning posthumously.

I wanted to know how long the coppery scent of the deer's blood clung to John's nostrils, what the warm, slick blood felt like as it flowed over his fast moving hands.

When John suggested that he would take me fishing for crappies, I was excited. I'd get to meet John, spend time in nature with him and learn something new. I'd never caught a fish before.

(Text) "I guarantee you will catch a lot of crappie, beginners always do," he'd promised.

John knew I was Covid concerned, that I had not been within six feet of anyone since March—not to go shopping, not even my children had come into my living space. When he suggested I ride in the back of his pickup so I wouldn't be in close proximity to him, I felt relieved.

(Text) "Will there be a tarp in the back so I can hide under it? We wouldn't want the highway patrol to spot me," I'd replied jokingly.

(Text) "Lol. I have a shell on the back. It's comfortable there and my dog can ride with you, if you'd like?"

Today was an amazingly beautiful late October day. John's pickup pulled up in front of my house just as the sun was beginning to move past pink spaces and into blue ones.

(Text) "I am outside! Bennett is excited to meet you, too!"

I grabbed the small bag of snacking items I'd pulled together the night before, plunked my new beige cap on my head for sunburn protection, picked up a light jacket and jogged down my driveway.

I suddenly felt awkward, shy about our first meeting. I couldn't see John's face, but I could see glimpses of his legs and boots as he moved along the driver's side of his vehicle to pop open the back of his pickup's shell.

I shimmied my way into the back of the shell and was delighted when his dog, Bennett, greeted me with friendly, soulful eyes and a wagging tail.

I'm lying face down in the most beautiful lake I've ever seen. Crappies drift by intent on their daily intake of young bass, perch and bluegills, along with mosquitoes and fathead minnows. I see the entrails John removed from my body lying closeby on the narrow shoreline.

Scavenger birds have started to take notice. I watch my body begin to turn blue, my hair is floating in the direction of a slight undertow. I watch for another minute or two before I drift away within the breeze of a perfectly lovely autumn day.

Servant Of The State:
Brian Daldorph

What do you need me to do?" I ask. "I'll do anything for my country, I believe that my record shows that."

If there's any type of hesitation on my part, I'll open myself up to charges of sedition that will almost certainly mean months or years in a labor camp. I've seen strong young men turn old after 12 months in a camp. They emerge stooped, toothless, broken.

I'm talking to one of the party's apparatchiks who plans to show his bosses how tough he is by kicking around an old writer with questionable party loyalty and too many friends outside the country.

"Your latest play," he says. "Quite wonderful in every way, well, in almost every way. But there are certain scenes and lines that the Committee sees as almost seditious in their veiled criticisms of our glorious state and might well be interpreted as aiding our enemies in their campaigns of hate against us."

He slides a few stapled pages across the desk to me with lines and scenes marked and the Committee of National Celebration's comments printed underneath.

"Far be it from us to criticize the work of a Master of the stage, a great writer honored by the state, but we would like you to revisit these lines and, if you deem it necessary, cut or revise them. I think you'll agree that this nation has been kind to you and the Committee hopes to see that kindness continue."

This bright boy will go far, there's no doubt about that. He's willing to do his bosses' bidding so he'll rise through the ranks until some rival will see him as a threat and eliminate him. He's sure he has power over me, but I have the strength and wiles of the survivor.

"Of course I will revise, revise, revise, and I'd like it on record that I thank the Committee for their diligence in this matter."

This apparatchik has arrogance and ambition that will destroy him.

I shake his cold hand on my way out.

BRIAN DALDORPH teaches at the University of Kansas and Douglas County Jail. He edits *Coal City Review*. His most recent books of poetry are *Ice Age/Edad de Hielo* (Irrupciones P, 2017), *Blue Notes* (Dionysia P, 2019), and *Kansas Poems* (Meadowlark P, 2021).

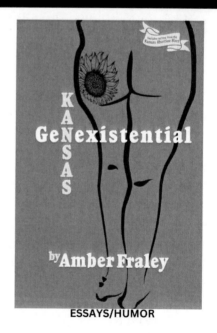

Letter From Hell:
Leonard Krishtalka

January 11, 1778

Carolus Linnaeus
Botanical Garden
Uppsala University
Uppsala, Sweden

My dear Carolus,

I was just informed of your death yesterday, January 10, 1778. And I was told that you are in Heaven. Well, you should know that I am in Hell.

And it is you I blame!

The authorities here in The Netherworld are allowing me this one privilege to write to you, but only after I had to explain your esteemed standing in the biological world to these ignoramuses. They knew nothing of your Systema Naturae, your classification of the life of the planet, of all living plants and animals inhabiting God's earth and waters.

How, you might ask, did I, your friend Anders Celsius, end up in Hell? The short answer is rank insubordination.

Here is the longer story. As you know, I died in the spring of 1744. When I came before St. Peter, I fully expected to be ushered into Heaven in reward for my discoveries about the astronomy of the heavens. After all, two years earlier, in the service of the Almighty, I had described the Centigrade thermometer at the gathering of the Swedish Academy of Sciences.

St. Peter welcomed me and proceeded to go through his spiel—the bounties of Heaven, the brutality of Hell. He made a special point of telling me, and I quote, "the temperature in Hell is 800 degrees Fahrenheit."

I was dumbfounded. "FAHRENHEIT!" I exploded at him. "YOU ARE MEASURING THE TEMPERATURE OF HELL IN FAHRENHEIT! NOT CENTIGRADE? Are you imbeciles? Nincompoops? The holy scriptures advertise you, St. Peter, as all knowing. Hah!"

St. Peter began to raise his hand, but I continued my outrage. "It's clear, St. Peter, you and your cohorts know nothing about the science of temperature. The Fahrenheit scale is a vulgar instrument, an insult to numerical grace—imagine water boiling at 212 degrees and freezing at 32 degrees. My Centigrade thermometer has mathematical elegance: water boils at 0 degrees and freezes at one 100 degrees."

What can I say, Carolus. St. Peter doesn't suffer insult or insubordination gladly. He raised his hand, tut-tutted, and tossed me into this underworld with the rest of the rogues here.

But not before he told me—with much glee, I might add—that none other than you, my dear Linnaeus, betrayed me after my death. You reversed my centigrade scale! Now water boils at 100 degrees and freezes at 0 degrees. St. Peter even gave me the citation. You published a scientific paper on December 16, 1745, in which you used what you called the "forward centigrade scale" to describe the temperature inside the greenhouse at the Botanical Garden of Uppsala University.

Here in Hell we have daily, mandatory sessions on penance. They tell me that I should forgive you, even thank you. It is true, I now admit in hindsight, that you made my Centigrade temperature scale a worldwide standard. Centigrade measures the glories of science and the tedium of the weather. Celsius, my name, is now also a household name, surpassing your own. "Degrees C" is ubiquitous, omnipresent, in all publications and announcements. My body might be in Hell, Carolus, but you have promoted my name to Heaven.

You need not take the time to answer this letter. We are not permitted to receive mail in Hell. Indeed, Hell has no paper. Where, you ask, did I purloin the two sheets for this missive to you? A recent arrival from America—which, like Hell, has adopted Fahrenheit—somehow managed to smuggle them in. He is one of us, a natural philosopher, a paleontologist, a former director of a natural history museum. He, of course, knows of you, and is well versed in your taxonomic tome.

But he will not tell me why he was sentenced to Hell. What I must tell you, though, is that he curses you daily. Why, you ask? Because in your Systema Naturae, you classified Canadian people not as Homo sapiens, but as "Homo monstrosus, head flattened." As you might imagine, he is a Canadian.

Your friend in Hell,
Anders Celsius

LEONARD KRISHTALKA has two parallel careers. As a professional paleontologist he has led and worked on expeditions in Canada, the US, China, Patagonia, Kenya and Ethiopia. As a prolific author, he has written award winning essays, the acclaimed book *Dinosaur Plots*, the Harry Przewalski detective novels, and *The Body on the Bed,* a work of historical fiction about murder and a sensational trial amid the social upheaval of post-Civil War Kansas.

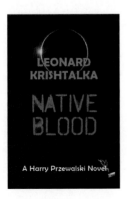

MAUREEN CARROLL

Duck Race:

Kevin Rabas

A Ten Minute Play

CHARACTERS:

CJ: 30s-40s, Nightclub owner and manager, bandleader, and jazz musician. Drummer.

TARA: 30s-40s: English Professor. Concentration: The Romantics.

TIME + PLACE:

Present Day. Somewhere in Kansas or Missouri.

PROPS:

Provided by the actors:

—rubber duck

—plastic skull

Necessary, but not provided by the actors:

—something to cover the skull, such as a jacket, a black towel, something.

Optional:

—A bed sheet, preferably blue or white (to symbolize a river).

—Although the duck and skull could be "pulled" down the river with black thread or fishing line, I think it might be much simpler to have someone "whisk" the duck and skull away by hand, once they are placed on the stage "in the river."

A STREAM. A blue or white SHEET, wavy on the stage floor, could symbolize a stream or the stream could just be imagined.

TARA enters, cradling a RUBBER DUCK. She walks to the edge of the stream, pauses, then crouches. She hesitates.

TARA

Please, please, please, float fast. I really need this win.

She reaches to put her duck in the water, but pauses, hearing CJ. CJ enters.

CJ:

A little downstream, don't you think?

TARA:

Oh.

CJ:

It's ok. I won't tell. Put 'er in.

TARA:

Ok. Promise you won't tell.

CJ:

Just tell me what number you are.

TARA:

What number?

CJ:

That way we'll both know, when you win.

TARA:

One hundred and two.

CJ:

That your only duck?

TARA:

Yes.

CJ:

Hope you win. Better put 'er in.

TARA:

(placing her duck in the water) Please, please, win.

CJ:

First year?

TARA:

First and last.

CJ:

How many ducks do you think are out there, floating around?

TARA:

Too many. Seven hundred. By last count.

CJ:

How do you know?

TARA:

They print it in the paper. Plus, if you look, you can see them coming. See them? See them there upstream?

CJ:

You don't seem like a regular crook or cheater. First time?

TARA:

Desperate times.

CJ:

Want to tell me, while the ducks float by?

TARA:

Ok. But we must first introduce ourselves. I'm Tara.

CJ:

CJ.

TARA:

Does it stand for something or were you always simply initials?

CJ:

It's actually Brandon Oliver Johnson.

TARA:

Where's the C?

CJ:

Well, I started with BJ, but you can image how that went over when I was a kid.

TARA:

Boys.

CJ:

Then OJ. But then that all went down.

TARA:

Oh.

CJ:

My father's name is Curtis. So I adopted the C.

TARA:

What do you do?

CJ:

Club owner and manager. And bandleader. Musician.

TARA:

What kind?

CJ:

Jazz mainly. Black American Music. At Room Indigo. You've heard of it? [shifting focus]

What's the winning pool up to?

TARA:

Twenty-two thousand.

CJ:

For one duck?

TARA:

For any number of ducks. But one wins.

CJ:

How much to enter?

TARA:

Twenty bucks.

CJ:

Why so desperate?

TARA:

I'm losing my job.

CJ:

Good one?

TARA:

Only thing I'm any good at. I teach.

CJ:

High school?

TARA:

College.

CJ:

Don't those who teach college have some sort of safeguard, some way that keeps them from not losing their jobs?

TARA:

Tenure?

CJ:

Tenure! Have it?

TARA:

Yes. It didn't work. It didn't work this time. The state suspended it. They cut 33 of us all at once.

CJ:

You a good teacher?

TARA:

Was.

CJ:

Can't you just go on the market?

TARA:

The market is hard. The schools pump out the PhDs. Without the jobs.

CJ:

Married?

TARA:

Was once. He left me for a much better scholar. I like to write, but I LOVE to teach.

CJ:

What subject?

TARA:

The Romantics.

CJ:

Sounds kind of hot.

TARA:

It's not really. "Romantics" with an upper-case "R." Dreamers more than lovers, except for Byron. And maybe Percy Shelley.

CJ:

I think I might have--

TARA:

But let's not talk about them. They were mainly miserable, passionate men. And a few women. One, Mary Shelley, did her writers group homework and wrote FRANKENSTEIN. The guys just SAID they would write something. But she DID it.

Something lasting. Something grand.

CJ:

How's your duck doing?

TARA:

Still ahead.

CJ:

Too far ahead to draw attention?

TARA:

Here come the others.

CJ:

Can't you do something?

TARA:

I could lecture, but I'd be so swamped with Composition

One papers that I'd lose my mind. Plus, it doesn't pay much. Not hardly enough. And I have my nephew living with me. And my Mom.

CJ:

But how could the university do this?

TARA:

Those high up the line think a major in English isn't worth much, isn't worth anything. It just doesn't pay. But it teaches you how to read deeply. How to think.

CJ:

Fight the power.

TARA:

Yes. And that.

CJ:

What will you do?

TARA:

I may tutor a few. And wait tables. If not for this duck.

CJ:

Good luck, duck. [to the duck] Go on. Go on.

TARA:

Too late, I think. They've caught up. I'm in the middle.

CJ:

But you had a lead.

TARA:

Isn't that how it always is. Why are you here?

CJ:

I like to watch. And I have another reason.

TARA;

Do tell.

CJ:

I like to spice it up.

TARA:

How?

He pulls a SKULL out from under cover: a coat, a blanket, something.

TARA:

What!

CJ:

[Taking the skull and placing it in the water] I like to mix it up a little. To me, it's better for the ducks.

TARA:

Better?

CJ:

Gives them something to think about. Something to keep them swimming.

TARA:

"Alas, poor Yorick."

CJ:

Yes. And that. It all comes for us. Sometime.

TARA:

I don't want to die a waitress. It's what I did as a kid.

CJ:

You're smart. Young enough.

TARA:

You wish.

CJ

Try something else.

TARA

I wish. [brief pause] We'll see. You know, with that skull, you really are a revolutionary.

CJ

Shouldn't we all be?

TARA

Yes. I guess. Yes.

CJ

How's your duck doing?

TARA

He's behind. Ten or twenty caught up and are outpacing him. I think my guy's in a spin.

CJ

It's ok. It's only one duck.

TARA

But it's my duck. And I intend to win.

CJ

Maybe my skull will scare some sense into him.

TARA

Have you always been a musician?

CJ

Yes. It's what I do. What I love.

TARA

What do you play?

CJ

Drums.

TARA

Drummers lead bands?

CJ

Yes. Art Blakey. Tony Williams. Yes. Yes, we do.

TARA

That skull your only reason for coming? To mix it up?

CJ

Well. I didn't tell you the whole thing. I'm not JUST a revolutionary.

TARA

Well?

CJ

I lost someone.

TARA

A girl?

CJ

The first lady to hire me. Gone.

TARA

Bandleader? You mourn a bandleader with a shiny white skull?

CJ

Not just that. She taught me everything.

TARA

Including love?

CJ

Including love. But she said, "Let's stay professional." And so I showed my love through the ride cymbal pattern, something to dance or glide to; and through the steady hi-hat "chick" on two and four; and through the subtle snare drum taps, rumbling and rolling beneath her golden voice.

TARA

So a skull?

CJ

So I wanted something. A sort of goodbye.

TARA

Send her down the river?

CJ

I had to. I had to send a kind of gift. For her.

TARA

A plastic skull. In the water?

CJ

So it seems.

TARA

I hope she sees how many ways you loved her. And I hope I win a month or two to regroup. You know, I'd like to come hear you.

CJ

Room Indigo is not far.

TARA

Ok. Save a seat for me. [brief pause] Save me something up front.

(Lights dim and go out. End of play.)

Kevin Rabas, http://kevinrabas.com/ Past Poet Laureate of Kansas (2017-2019) Kevin Rabas teaches at Emporia State University, where he leads the poetry and playwriting tracks in the Department of English, Modern Languages, and Journalism. He is a seventh generation Kansan. He has fourteen books, including Lisa's Flying Electric Piano, a Kansas Notable Book and Nelson Poetry Book Award winner. He is the recipient of the Emporia State President's and Liberal Arts & Sciences Awards for Research and Creativity, and he is the winner of the Langston Hughes Award for Poetry

2023 Finalists
THE AMITY LITERARY PRIZE
by Anamcara Press

Thaddeus Duggon, *A Record of Change*

Beth Gullley, *Frog Joy*

Debra Irisk, *Life Moments*

J.A. McGovern, *Words Left Unspoken*

Interview With An Artist

DIANA DUNKLEY—ARTIST AND ILLUSTRATOR

— BY MICKI CARROLL

MC: Are you originally from Kansas?

DD: I was born in Washington, DC, but moved to Kansas when I was three, so almost. My father was born in Lawrence in 1897, so I have very deep roots here.

MC: Is there anything special about your art studio or space or process that you think helps you?

DD: I made the decision years ago to have a studio in Lawrence instead of at my farm home so I wouldn't be distracted by all the things that need to be done at home. It was practical in being much larger and more accessible for teaching classes, as well as providing a more professional space for me to present my work to gallerists and potential clients. These days I am not as inclined to have people in my space, so I have innumerable projects spread out all over that I am working on and - I don't have to clean them up every night!

MC: Can you tell about an early experience where you learned that art had power?

DD: My second year at KU as a sculpture major I took a class from newly recruited instructor, George Tuton. There were only two people in the advanced sculpture class and the in the first session George asked us what we planned to do. I was so shocked I didn't know how to respond. I asked, "Do you mean we can do anything we want to do?" He replied yes, and I said "Can I get back to you on that?" From that moment I learned that art could be anything you choose it to be. It can be an event that is the actual artwork, documented or not. It

can be an expression to instigate social change. It can also be more traditional forms, which I also practice. However, as a sophomore at KU, that interaction gave me the freedom to pursue my dreams and explore my beliefs. My most current artwork the Respect Among All Things project is directly derived from that freedom. It is a collaborative ongoing project that is made up of many approaches and collaborations around that concept, some of which are workshops, discussions, musical compositions, yard signs - and just about anything anyone feels inspired to pursue around the topic. It will be available soon on three websites: respectamongallthings.com, .org and .net. respectamongallthings.net will be dedicated to an International Graffiti Competition.

MC: What do you enjoy most about creating art?

DD: Influencing the energies in the universe around it.

MD: What would you say is the most difficult part of creating art?

DD: The most difficult part of creating art for me by far is to reach down into the depths of what isn't always easy or comfortable and bring my true self into the artwork. I also feel that this is an essential element in my art.

MC: What is something surprising you learn about yourself through creating art?

DD: I learn new things about myself and lots of other things every day through my art! One of my favorite parts of creating is researching a concept. I did learn how much perfectionism can ruin my art when the pandemic was happening and I felt like I had to control my artwork. I suffered from what I ended up naming Pandemic Perfectionist Paralysis, meaning I couldn't create because it was never perfect. I got rid of that attitude, thank goodness!

MC: Do you hide any secrets in your artwork that only a few people will find?

DD: Of course! (Wink)

MC: Do you view art creation as a kind of spiritual practice?

DD: Absolutely. I have certain rituals and meditations that I use in my art practice, as well as the essence of flow that it provides me and sends out to anything that will receive it.

MC: How many hours a day / week do you "do art"?

DD: I come into my studio for at least 5 and usually more hours a day, 6 days a week. I am usually focused on art activities, but that can be like answering questions for this interview or even paying bills. Just because I am there doesn't mean that I am in creating mode, but at least I am showing to do the work if it is possible. The COVID Pandemic really damaged my creative energy, but since the first of this year I have been steadily reclaiming it and finally am feeling like myself again,.

MC: If you didn't do art, what would you do?

DD: I would be dead.

MC: Do you want each piece to stand on its own, or are you trying to build a body of work with connections between each creation?

DD: I work both ways - sometimes as a one-off and sometimes in series. However, because they are all my creations and have my stylistic "mark" on them, there is some continuity in all work that I do - whether it be painting, printmaking, drawing, installation, performance or conceptual art.

MC: Do you have relationships with other artists? How do you support each other?

DD: As an artist and an introvert, I have been very fortunate to have belonged to several artist groups that have been focused on support and encouragement. I love nothing more than a good art collaboration, whether it be with one other person, an entire community or the whole of the Cosmos! Currently I am involved with an international artist collaboration named The Pleiades Project, that consists of 4 artists in the US and 3 artists in Australia. We have been collaborating and creating together since 2014 and are planning another in-person exhibit in Australia in 2024-25. I also hang out with several wonderful artists who trust each other with their artistic vulnerabilities and feel comfortable sharing and discussing difficult topics.

MC: Do you finish everything you create?

DD: Of course not!

MC: What happens to old starts?

DD: Sometimes I paint over them with black gesso. Sometimes I burn them (finished pieces too). Sometimes I forget about them. I have notebooks and sketchbooks full of ideas that have barely been started.

MC: Do you have any recommendations for young or aspiring artists?

DD: I was not the best nor the most talented artist as I was growing up, but I was the most driven and

I worked hard. Try your best to not compare your artwork or yourself to other artists, and don't give up!

Diana Dunkley Is a full-time artist working out of Studio 3D in Lawrence, KS USA for over 40 years. Diana received a B.F.A. from the University of Kansas with a double degree in Sculpture and Interior Design. Dunkley's work is shown nationally and internationally, including exhibitions in Ottawa, Canada and Sydney and Katoomba, Australia. Dunkley has also exhibited in multiple solo and group exhibitions throughout their career, and is in collections around the globe.

Recently, Dunkley participated in an exhibition at the Lawrence Arts Center with the collaborative group, "The Pleiades Project: an International Art Collaboration" involving seven artists: 3 from Australia and 4 from the USA. This collaboration has been ongoing since 2015, with plans for another group exhibition in Australia in 2024.

Dunkley's current project is titled Respect Among All Things and will be represented on-line at respectamongallthings.com. It is an ongoing conceptual artwork that features many collaborations, artworks, art events and art workshops based on the title concept.

LEONARD KRISHTALKA

Hard-Boiled Detective Series Mixes Bones, Murder & History!

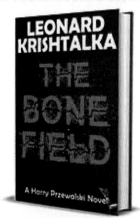

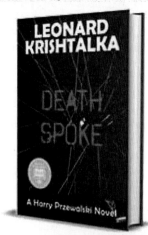

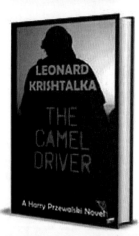

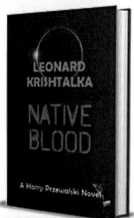

The Harry Przewalski Series

Bookstores Carrying
The Write Bridge Journal

Ad Astra Books & Coffee House, 135 N Santa Fe Ave, Salina KS 67501, 785-833-2235

Books & Burrow, 212 S Broadway st., PItttsburg KS 66762 (620) 238-5330

Chapters Books & Gifts, 548 Seward Street, Seward, NE 68434; 402-643-2282

Crow & Co. Books, 2 S Main St., Hutchinson KS 67501, 620-500-5200

The Nook, 703 8th Street, Baldwin City, KS 66006 (785) 594-2526

The Raven Bookstore, 809 Massachusetts St, Lawrence, KS 66044, (785) 749-3300

Rivendell Bookstore, 212 N Broadway St, Abilene, KS 67410; (785) 571-5001

Roundtable bookstore, 826 N Kansas Ave, Topeka, KS 66608; (785) 329-5366

Twice Told Tales, 104 S Main St, McPherson KS 67460 620-718-5023

Watermark Books & Café, 4701 E Douglas, Wichita, KS 67218; (316) 682-1181. www.watermarkbooks.com

*Ask your local bookstore to carry **The Write Bridge** Journal!*

Resources for Mid-West Writers

ARTISTS & ILLUSTRATORS

Bobbie Powell, bobbielynpowell@gmail.com, https://www.facebook.com/php?id=10064184227637

Cathy Martin, McLouth, Kansas, cymn4art@gmail.com

Amanda McCollum, Overland Park, Kansas.

Diana Dunkley, Studio 3D, 1019 Delaware St., Lawrence, Kansas USA 66044, ddunkleyat3d@earthlink.net

PRINTERS

KC Book Manufacturing Co. 110 W 12th Ave, Kansas City, MO 64116; (816) 842-9770

Bookmobile, 210 Edge Place, Minneapolis, MN 55418,

Gasch Printing, 1780 Crossroads Dr, Odenton, MD 21113

Oklahoma Bindery, Inc., 2832 W. Lindley, Oklahoma City, OK 73107

Mennonite Press, Inc., 532 N. Oliver Road, Newton, KS 67114, BetterSelf-Publishing.com 800-536-4686

Thanks To Our Sponsors:

Chad Broughman

Pat Clevelant

Amber Fraley

George Gurley

KC Book Manufacturing Co.

Kathleen Kaska

Leonard Krishtalka

Ronda Miller

Patrick Sumner

Mark Wolfson